SPIRITUAL ENTREPRENEURSHIP

Raw reflections of a female CEO

SHERI A. SMITH, M.A.

Copyright © 2023 Sheri A. Smith
All rights reserved.
ISBN: 9798378596768
Independently published

For Spiritual Entrepreneurship resources visit:
https://www.bridgingheartsfoundation.org/

Dedication

This book is dedicated to my parents,
Allen and Debra Burnham. Their union was miraculous in nature,
and they dedicated me to God as a baby.

The foundation my parents built was instrumental in my desire to become a spiritual entrepreneur and share my journey with others.

In my toughest times, they supported me and always sought to do their best. Mom and Dad pray for my sister and me every day. Dad sounds the *shofar* for us and the world.

Their actions have greater spiritual implications than can be known.

Thank you for your love!

Note: After the book was launched, my sweet momma passed away unexpectedly on July 3, 2023. I feel incredibly fortunate that she had the opportunity to read the book. Mom is still supporting our collective spiritual entrepreneurship endeavors from heaven. It's as if she has assembled a committee of angels to provide us with encouragement and cheer us on!

TABLE OF CONTENTS

ACKNOWLEDGMENTS   i

INTRODUCTION   1

Chapter 1. The Backstory Behind this Book   7

    1. My Spiritual Context   9
        a. Religion growing up   10
        b. Choosing legalism over love   12
        c. On leaving my faith   13
        d. New beginnings   15
        e. Founding Indigo   16

    2. Conclusion: How Indigo Became the Impetus for this Book   19

Chapter 2. The Three Dimensions of Spiritual Entrepreneurship   21

    1. My Evolving Entrepreneurial Journey   21
        a. Entrepreneurship   22
        b. Social entrepreneurship   22
        c. Spiritual entrepreneurship   24

    2. The Three Dimensions of Spiritual Entrepreneurship   26
        a. First dimension: Founder Focus   29
            i. The role of fear and resistance   31
            ii. Your journey is not just about you   33
        b. Second dimension: Employee Focus   34
        c. Third dimension: Business Focus   39
            i. Organizational development models   41
            ii. The tension of a spiritual enterprise: redefining control and success   46
            iii. The tension of a spiritual enterprise: revealing light from darkness   48

    3. Conclusion: Putting It All Together with Integrative Ability   50
        a. Integrating the masculine and feminine   50

Chapter 3. The Three Principles of Venture Capital — 55

   1. The three principles of venture capital align to our failing education system — 57

   2. Exclusivity — 59
      a. Exclusivity in venture capital — 63
      b. Increasing equity and reducing bias through inclusivity — 65

   3. Ranking and Sorting — 66
      a. Enoughness replacing ranking and sorting — 68

   4. Money — 69
      a. Self-interest and wetiko — 71
      b. Social impact investing in its current form is not the answer — 73
      c. We can't help but focus on the wealthy — 74
      d. Money follows existing power structures — 75
      e. Funding alternatives to institutional capital — 77
      f. Spiritual capital redefines value — 80

   5. Conclusion: Refocusing Humanity's ROI — 81

Chapter 4. Valuing the Intrinsic — 85

   1. An Axiological Model for Spiritual Entrepreneurship — 86
      a. Overvaluing the systemic — 91
      b. Overvaluing the extrinsic — 92
         i. Extrinsic interactions vs. intrinsic connection — 95
      c. The intrinsic as the focus of spiritual entrepreneurship — 97
         i. Spiritual entrepreneurship is about people — 99

   2. Conclusion: Balancing the Intrinsic, Extrinsic, and Systemic — 101

Chapter 5. Rules of the Road — 105

   1. Mentorship and Spiritual Entrepreneurship — 106
      a. Co-creation as a pathway forward — 108
      b. Honoring all forms of learning — 110
      c. The co-creation circle — 111

   2. Knowing and Spiritual Entrepreneurship — 113
      a. Mind knowing vs. cellular knowing — 114

   3. Decision Making and Spiritual Entrepreneurship — 116
      a. Decision-making: business planning — 116
      b. Decision-making: saying yes — 120

c. Decision-making: saying no	121
i. Do not second guess your decisions	122
d. Decision-making: multi-generational focus	123
4. Profits and Spiritual Entrepreneurship	125
5. Pricing and Spiritual Entrepreneurship	128
a. "Free" as a pricing strategy	130
b. The rise of freemium pricing models	131
c. My personal story of "free"	132
i. A world without Santa Clause	133
ii. Vacation Bible schools and free museum days	134
iii. The joy of a library and free pizza	135
d. The greatest things in life really are free	136
e. Pricing to maximize value	136
6. Exits and Spiritual Entrepreneurship	137
a. The currency of heaven is love	138
7. Conclusion: Being on the Path is Enough	140

Chapter 6. Tools of the Trade — **141**

1. Prayer as a Business Tool for Spiritual Entrepreneurs	141
a. Prayers we use regularly	143
b. Movement prayers	146
c. Meditation	147
d. Prayer in business	149
2. Empathy as a Business Tool for Spiritual Entrepreneurs	149
a. Empaths	150
b. Empathy in business	152
3. Surrender as a business tool for spiritual entrepreneurs	156
a. Surrender in business	158
4. Discernment as a Business Tool for Spiritual Entrepreneurs	159
a. Discernment vs. Judgment	160
b. Breathing	161
c. Body-based discernment	162
d. Emotional discernment	164
e. Discernment is a practice, not a destination	165
f. Discernment in business	166
5. Conclusion: Use the Tools that Call to You	168

Chapter 7. Self-Development for the Spiritual Entrepreneur — 169

    1. The Paradox of Self-Help — 171

    2. The Four Stages of Self-Development — 172
        a. The first stage is Know Yourself — 173
        b. The second stage is Choose Yourself — 175
        c. The third stage is Create Yourself — 177
        d. The fourth stage is Give Yourself — 180
            i. Energy and giving yourself — 181
            ii. Loving yourself to give yourself — 183

    3. Conclusion: The Self-Development Model in Action for Spiritual Entrepreneurs — 184
        a. The cycle of rebirth — 186

Chapter 8. Revealing the Kingdom of Heaven on Earth — 189

    1. Seeing with our hearts — 190
        a. Growing diversity — 191

    2. Driving innovation with freedom — 192

    3. Collective, community-based action — 194

    4. Choosing the intrinsic path — 195

    5. Conclusion: The Kingdom of Heaven is Among Us — 196
        a. Expanding love in liminal space — 198
        b. Look at your life through heaven's eyes — 200

Appendix I. Chapter Discussion Questions — 201

Appendix II. Descriptions of the Prayers — 211

    1. The Lord's Prayer — 212

    2. Praise Prayer — 213

    3. Jeanne Guyon's Prayer — 215

    4. Ho'oponopono Prayer — 216

    5. The Eight-Step Prayer — 222

Appendix III: Bibliography — 229

ACKNOWLEDGMENTS

"For Good" from the hit musical *Wicked* has always been an anthem of forgiveness and gratitude for me. The lyrics beautifully capture the idea that the people we encounter can have a lasting impact on us, shaping who we are and the paths we take.

> I've heard it said
> That people come into our lives
> For a reason
> Bringing something we must learn
> And we are led
> To those who help us most to grow
> If we let them
> And we help them in return
> Well, I don't know if I believe that's true
> But I know I'm who I am today
> Because I knew you.[1]

As I write this acknowledgment, I am grateful for the many people who have played a role in bringing this book to fruition. Of course, it is impossible to mention everyone who has impacted my life "for good," but I want to highlight a few individuals who have played a significant role in the process.

---

[1] "For Good," *Wicked* (Decca Broadway, 2003).

First, I want to acknowledge everyone who has been part of Indigo over the past ten years—our board, advisors, investors, partners and customers. You are the lifeblood of this work: your contributions release sparks of the divine in the mundane. My current team moves mountains daily, and I love co-creating with all of you.

Thank you to Lauren and Richard Michalka for helping me with the cover and reading one of the very first manuscripts. Blessings to Kath Gabutero for spending countless hours sorting out the footnotes and bibliography and for Kim Marques facilitating the many meetings necessary to publish this book while still navigating my work at Indigo. Deep gratitude to Sueann Casey for witnessing my spiritual journey for more than twenty years now and for loving the core of me no matter what I believed.

Next, I'd like to express a huge thank you to Chris Howard. You edited this book countless times and wrestled with me through many murky sections. Your talent is a gift and a kindness to me. Also, thank you to Sydney Wiederhold and Breanna Armand for supporting the editing efforts—much of this text was incoherent in its early stages and you tackled it beautifully.

The Hartman Institute Wisdom Council members Art Ellis and Steve Byrum were instrumental in supporting me on the chapters discussing axiology. Other devotees of Hartman's work have shaped my thinking and inclusion of his fundamental concepts, including Renee Wood, Rem Edwards, and Cliff Hurst.

I dedicated this book to my parents, who have always encouraged me to be my true self. Thank you to my dear sister, Pamela Tellado, who walked with me throughout our lives. She never wavered in faith and always treated me with grace. It was complete joy to receive Pam's endorsement of the work.

Sending love to my friend and spiritual brother John Lee—you and I have spent innumerable hours discussing spiritual entrepreneurship for years, before we even knew the term. I've only begun to incorporate your insights and suggestions. I appreciate you so much.

I also want to acknowledge the board and members of the Washington, DC, Church of the Holy City, who brought me Swedenborg's writings and the concept of spiritual entrepreneurship, especially Reverend Rich Tafel, who gave me the idea for the book. Malcom Peck, Kateryna Pyatybratova, Annabel Park, and Cheryl Robertson have all contributed to this effort.

Thank you, Vince Jordan, for opening my heart to Jewish teachings almost a decade ago and teaching me to recognize the Almighty One in all things. Rabbi Elan Babchuck, I am grateful for your work with the Glean Network to support Spiritual Entrepreneurs and for your review and endorsement of this book. I also appreciate Rabbi Yoel Glick for sharing Jewish Meditation with me and revealing insights on the divine feminine Shekhinah energy.

Finally, I deeply appreciate all the early readers, who were willing to provide feedback and encouragement. Thank you Ron Bonnstetter, Michael Sheller, Jillian Perkins, Dave and Jody Hodges, Brenda Wentworth, John Garrott, Steven Myers, Rehan Dawer, Ted Zoller, Greg Jackson, Summer Smith, Christin Myrick, Cybelle Lyon, Jason Schrock, Kenneth Young, Matt Willmott, Dameon Alexander, Shala Graham, Doug Smith, Sue Gleeson, Heather Blackbird, Walter Balser, and Deidre Gwin. Those of you who are mentioned in the book, thank you for being willing to share your insights. By the time this book is published, I'm sure there will be more early readers not mentioned here—know that I appreciate your contributions.

Each and every one of you has influenced me "for good." This book is as much a reflection of your impact on my life as it is of my own experiences and insights. So, to all of you, I say thank you. Thank you for your guidance, support, and unwavering belief in me. This book would not exist without you, and for that, I am forever grateful.

INTRODUCTION

The purpose of this book is to explore the idea of spiritual entrepreneurship through my journey as a female education technology (EdTech) CEO.

Spiritual entrepreneurship is still a relatively new concept. There aren't many widely accepted definitions. I don't believe that spiritual entrepreneurship should be too narrowly defined because language is notoriously bad at describing spiritual notions. I think of a spiritual entrepreneur as **someone who runs an enterprise with the purpose of expanding love, not extracting gain.**

Spiritual entrepreneurs operate with the tension of having to deliver material products or services while maintaining a focus on non-material aspects of humanity. They are constantly holding the three primary dimensions of founder, employee, and business with simultaneous focus on:

1. Personal growth
2. Development of others
3. Elevation of human consciousness and/or revealing the kingdom of heaven on earth via their enterprise's mission[1]

---

[1] I use these two seemingly divergent ideas synonymously. They are meant to describe the same idea from different perspectives.

Chapter two discusses the origins of the definition and the three dimensions of spiritual entrepreneurship at length.

Book goals

It is my intention that this book accomplishes the following:

- Broadens and clarifies the concept of a spiritual entrepreneur and spiritual entrepreneurship

- Shares insights and struggles from a person who identifies as a spiritual entrepreneur but is still in the process of figuring out what a spiritual entrepreneur is and does, and how spiritual entrepreneurship is approached

- Outlines some frameworks, ideas, and tools useful for others who identify as spiritual entrepreneurs

- Grows a conversation around this topic, helping to unite founders, investors, employees, and interested parties to further the growth of spiritual entrepreneurship

- Encourages the growth of intrinsic systems that allow for spiritual entrepreneurs to flourish

- Hastens the revelation of God's kingdom on earth through the efforts of the spiritual entrepreneurship community, which I hope will bless all people[2]

---

[2] Everyone must come to their own definition of what this means. In short, I define "God's kingdom on earth" as a world of peace with enough for everyone. Everyone is valued for who they are and has a place in society where each person works together to bring value to their community. We also respect the planet and all created things, restoring and protecting Mother Earth. Scripture describes it as living

INTRODUCTION

This book is not meant to be polished or perfect. It is not a formulaic self-help book or a road map. It does not promise health, wealth, or even wisdom. My goal is not to be perceived as an expert. I am simply a person doing my best to live God's will while learning every day how much I *don't* know. Not knowing is so integral to my current stage of life that I have recently made a radical commitment to it.[3] Not knowing is the first step in setting aside the ego, suspending judgment, and being opened to witnessing what God is doing in a larger context.

This book is also a moment in time. Indigo started in 2013, but it took me many years to begin consciously realizing that the nature of my journey was not characteristic of a typical entrepreneur, nor did I want it to be. That is why there seem to be many different topics at various stages of development contained within these chapters. This encourages me because it is real—the truth is humans are continually growing at various stages of development in different aspects of our lives. I want this book to reflect our imprecise human journey.

Chapter Summary

The outline and purpose of each chapter is briefly described next.

Chapter 1: The Backstory to This Book provides context about my life and spiritual journey so the reader can understand my perspective in writing this book.

---

with "one mind, one heart, dwelling in righteousness with no poor (physically, emotionally and spiritually) among us."

[3] "Not knowing" is one of the three core tenets of the Zen Peacemakers: Roshi Egyoku Nakao, "The Three Tenets," *Zen Peacemakers International*: https://zenpeacemakers.org/the-three-tenets/.

Chapter 2: The Three Dimensions of Spiritual Entrepreneurship explores the roles of the founder, the employees, and the company itself, illustrating their constant integration in the life of a spiritual entrepreneur.

Chapter 3: The Three Principles of Venture Capital contrasts the venture capital model with the three dimensions of spiritual entrepreneurship. This chapter highlights how venture capital's methods of exclusivity, ranking and sorting, and money are entirely divergent from spiritual entrepreneurship.

Venture Capital	**Spiritual Capital**
Exclusivity	Inclusivity
Ranking & Sorting	Enoughness
Money	Value

Chapter 4: Valuing the Intrinsic provides a framework for spiritual entrepreneurship that emphasizes intrinsic value. It describes how our inner and outer worlds are better understood through the importance we place on the intrinsic, extrinsic, and systemic.

Chapter 5: Rules for the Road discusses how the rules for spiritual entrepreneurs differ from the rules of traditional entrepreneurship. The chapter highlights common business areas and includes specific examples of how a spiritual entrepreneur can look at typical business ideas through another lens.

Traditional Entrepreneurs	Spiritual Entrepreneurs
Mentorship	Co-Creation
Mind Knowing	Cellular Knowing
Fact-Based Decision Making	Heart-Based Decision Making
Accomplishment Focused	Multi-Generational Focused
Expanding Profit	Expanding Love
Pricing to Maximize Profit	Pricing to Maximize Value
Unicorn Exit	Eternal Exit

Chapter 6: Tools of the Trade provides some resources that have been helpful on my journey: prayer, empathy, discernment, and surrender. It is not meant to be an all-inclusive toolkit, simply a starting point for discussion.

Chapter 7: Self-Development for the Spiritual Entrepreneur describes why self-development is essential for spiritual entrepreneurs, then it introduces a robust model by which we can engage in that process.

Chapter 8: Revealing the Kingdom of Heaven on Earth encourages spiritual entrepreneurs to work together to grow diversity, drive innovation with freedom, and see ourselves and others through heaven's eyes.

Appendix I: Discussion Questions provides a series of questions that can be used for facilitating powerful conversations. These discussion questions can be answered on your own or with a group of other entrepreneurs striving toward the same goals.

Appendix II: Prayers provides detailed instructions on the prayers from chapter 6.

Appendix III: Bibliography is a list of websites, articles, and books mentioned in the text.

Referring to "God" in the book

It is impossible to accurately describe the infinite Reality of love in our universe with language. However, after much consideration, I chose to use the word "God," the pronoun "he," and the term "Father" when referring to the Creator of the universe. This is because I come from a Christian tradition, and these are the most familiar terms to me. However, I want to emphasize that the term "God" is used inclusively and can be substituted with other words from your own tradition that represent the divine boundless One, beyond forms and names. I also believe that the concept of God must include both male and female qualities since God is All, and therefore a single pronoun for God is insufficient. I hope this explanation helps you understand my approach to discussing the divine in this book.

Contact Me!

I am eager to collaborate with more folks on this journey. Feel free to reach out to me with questions and comments by emailing Sheri@IndigoPathway.com. Join the mailing list on our non-profit website https://www.bridgingheartsfoundation.org/ and receive updates on spiritual entrepreneurs we are featuring on the site.

Chapter 1
The Backstory to this Book

Very rarely is a story written from the midst of the battle, where there are no clear-cut winners and losers and no exciting victory to entice the reader. We are programmed to want to know who won and who lost. We immediately give credit to the winner for being brilliant, brave, or smart. We love the overcoming story—the little guy who made it against all odds—but only if the little guy actually makes it. If the little guy hasn't made it yet, we have little interest in his day-to-day struggles, hopes, and dreams.

But there *is* value in telling a story from the perspective of the mundane, from the real perspective that many of us are in for most of our lives. If we are honest with ourselves, we are all in a state of *not knowing*: a state of barely making it, a state of feeling like we must keep up with some sort of rat race that is leading us nowhere, or a state of being in a cloud where we dutifully go through the motions each day feeling numb or hazy, unclear where we are going or what the point really is.

My stepdaughter attempted suicide when she was sixteen. As part of her healing journey, she wrote a book called *The Blue Journal*. Her book is one such "in between" story. It is a raw reflection, written amid struggling in order to heal a deep wound that may or may not ever completely resolve. I am so proud of her for having the courage to write that book. The effect of her story was to draw me closer to her, increasing the love we hold for each other. It is my prayer that the result of reading this book also increases love in our hearts.

This book is a moment in time. It is my story of the past ten years growing a small education company called Indigo. From one perspective, my efforts have largely failed. Few people would consider me successful from a financial standpoint. We've either lost money or barely broken even almost every year we've been in business (we did have a small profit last year).

From another perspective, we are wildly successful. Indigo is financially sustainable, has a wonderful product, a loyal customer base, and incredible team members. We receive emails regularly from people whose lives have been transformed because Indigo exists. People tell us that our emphasis on self-awareness and empowerment are desperately needed in education and our work is changing the world. Small miracles happen time and time again, and we are propelled along by some force that seems beyond us. We have only had the bare minimum in funding necessary to stay alive, but amazing opportunities often present themselves in ways we never would have dreamed.

As a business owner, the perspective of having a great product that changes lives, while not being able to sustain profits, is incredibly perplexing. The simultaneous holding of two opposite perspectives has been instrumental in my development as a leader. In fact, it is one of the central themes of this book: the tension of experiencing multiple realities in the same moment. The tension of holding two opposites that are both true at the same time is one of the great gifts of spiritual entrepreneurship and of being human. It is a gift because problem-solving in an interconnected global community requires people to maturely handle complexity and allow space for multiple perspectives without judgement (described as integrative ability in the next chapter).

Continuing to put forth the effort, which is by nature required of an entrepreneur, while these two opposites remain juxtaposed is difficult at best. If I didn't believe in something bigger than money, power, or success, I would have given up long ago. In April 2020, when we completely ran out of cash due to the pandemic, I considered shuttering the business. However, shortly after experiencing this quandary, I first heard the phrase "spiritual entrepreneur." And it refueled my hope to continue. Before describing the striking impact that phrase had on my life, though, I want to share a bit of context to help you understand where I'm coming from because perspective and context are crucial to understanding.

My Spiritual Context

I'm forty-two, and no one would describe me as having any remarkable talents, certainly not in the arts or on an athletic field. Growing up in rural Michigan in a lower-middle class family, I never really lacked for anything although my parents struggled financially for many years. Blessed with an ability to play the "school game," I received a high-end education in Washington, DC, and opportunities to travel the world. Despite external achievement, I've often been filled with angst, self-doubt, and painful feelings. This pain has driven me toward exploring deeper aspects of life that create meaning.

Since this book is about spiritual entrepreneurship, some of you may think that I consider myself to be especially spiritual or religious. I want to make it clear that I am not. Like everyone, I am on a spiritual journey that is evolving daily. And since this book is focused on spiritual principles, my personal faith story is included as context. I believe that:

- Spiritual entrepreneurs are present in all faiths, and many don't identify with any religion at all
- Heaven is for all who choose it
- Revealing the light of the divine is in the original design of every soul

James Headsten Barry, Staff Chaplain at Thomas Jefferson University Hospital, sums up the heart of the Christian philosophy as I currently view it:

> Unconditional love of the human race is the profound motivation behind why Christ was born. All people are universally included in the Divine plan of spiritual development, and none are excluded. This is so all people may be lifted up to understand, and then follow their highest purpose in life.[1]

Religion growing up

I grew up attending a tiny nondenominational country church in rural Michigan. We went three times per week and brought as many neighborhood kids as we could in our old station wagon. We went to pretty much every summer vacation Bible school in the county, and I also attended a Baptist youth group regularly.

My belief in God was deep and I often sensed God's presence but never could relate to the formality of church. I particularly detested preaching of any kind. I liked the singing, the community, the

---

[1] James H. Barry, correspondence with Rev. Rich Tafel, 2022.

potlucks, and the Bible. Jesus and his angels always seemed very real to me. The security I felt from believing that God cared about my life was reassuring.

For my senior year of high school, I went to live with my grandmother outside of Boston. She was a first-generation Italian American Catholic and only went to Mass on some holidays. While I was with her, I rather enjoyed being freed from the restrictions of church and the boredom of going multiple times a week. My church-free state continued through my first semester of college. As a college freshman at the ripe old age of seventeen, you would have thought I would experiment with what the world had to offer, but strangely I did not. I never drank, partied, or even swore. I was still as innocent as they come and remember being shocked when a boy kissed me for the first time on one of our pre-study jogs. Up to that point, I had always assumed boys would never like me.

During winter break in my freshman year at American University, I spent six weeks in Australia with a foreign exchange student that I had met in Michigan. She was an evangelical Christian, and we did lots of churchy activities while I was there. The most significant spiritual encounter on that trip was a magical sunrise on a southern Australian beach, where I literally felt completely merged with God, nature, and the world. Time stopped and we all became one.

I had a few vague recollections of feelings of "oneness" prior to age eight but had stuffed them far away because the memories were confusing. Then, years later on that Australian beach, I suddenly felt that God was calling me back and had a purpose for my life. My entire soul craved this relationship, and I became determined to find an avenue back to God when returning to the States.

Choosing legalism over love

In my "seeking," I jumped at the first religious opportunity that presented itself to me in the form of a Bible study in our school cafeteria. Unfortunately, this Bible study led me to become heavily involved in a legalistic, global church movement that many claim was a cult. Without delving much into my experiences in this cult-like church, I will say that I regret many of the things I said, did, and believed. I betrayed my deepest self because I so desperately wanted to fit in and because I wanted to do what I thought God required of me.

Among the leaders in the church, there was a practice that had an "arranged marriage" feel to it. Couples were strongly encouraged to marry if the church leaders believed that they had what it took to plant a church together. Because women were not allowed to preach and were severely limited in their roles without being married, there was a strong urgency to marry young in order to move up the leadership ladder.

By the time I was twenty-one and had graduated from college, I too was feeling that pressure. Consequently, I married someone I barely knew, nine years my senior. Despite serious misgivings and even saying no while crying hysterically when he proposed, I still married him. I believed him when he said, "God wants you to marry me," and almost immediately regretted it.

Within two years, I realized the whole world I'd built my life around was a sham. On my first visit to a local therapist, I proclaimed, "Either my husband's crazy or I'm crazy! I'm not sure what's real anymore." My meetings with her gave me the strength to pack up my bright red Toyota Echo, put my two 100-pound dogs in the back seat, and drive to Vail, Colorado, leaving behind an emotionally abusive church and husband.

There was good that came from these experiences, and I still have friends from that part of my journey today. In fact, Indigo's CXO, Sueann Casey, and I met while leading teen ministries in sister churches. The church split in the early 2000s and many of the remnant churches became lovely spiritual homes for good people. However, the judgment I developed, the feelings of self-righteousness, believing I knew better, and thinking there was only one true church had destroyed my sense of self and my ability to receive love on a level that is very hard to describe.

On leaving my faith

Having done "all the right things" and having been met with bitter disappointment, I decided to leave my faith. I still believed in God emotionally but abandoned specific allegiance to religion and religious ideas. In essence, I was an agnostic with faith in something bigger than myself. I rather liked this state of being. It was freeing. It was as if I had my agency back and I could decide what felt right or wrong for myself rather than being controlled by others. I didn't lose my sense of ethics or who I was; truthfully, it was the very opposite. It was like meeting myself for the first time. Exploring who I was in a new context was glorious and expansive. Unrestricted by imposed rules and regulations, I pushed the boundaries and discovered new facets of the human experience.

After a few years of a rather hedonistic lifestyle, however, I became bored and knew I needed a shift. I left Vail, a wonderful boyfriend, dear friends, and a fantastic job to finish my master's degree in Communication, Culture, and Technology at Georgetown—not because I liked school or needed the degree but because it felt like unfinished business. The unfinished work represented a leg of my journey that was unexpectedly interrupted when I married. Now twenty-eight years old, I felt compelled to retrace that path I had left at twenty-one and see what it had in store.

That year in DC, 2009, turned out to be the hardest year of my life. That path just felt empty. DC felt like a tomb. School was meaningless. I was racking up insane amounts of debt. A series of small, hard things ate at me, feeling like a continual stream of bad luck. I was depressed and felt hopeless. Being back in DC reminded me of the time in my life when I was caught up in legalistic religion, and it felt strange being back there without all of that. By this point, I knew I wanted to find my way back to God, to align myself with his will; I just had no idea how that could happen.

The bright spot of that year was attending a ten-month leadership program through the Coaches Training Institute.[2] During this program I met incredible friends, among them was Dr. Susan Gleeson, whom I now consider a spiritual mentor. Out of all the participants, Sue was the only one who identified as a Christian. I recall the time when she stood before us, her eyes shining with tears. She showed immense courage and vulnerability by admitting that she felt like she couldn't be her true self among us. Group members of other faiths were acknowledged and appreciated, whereas the word "Jesus" was almost considered taboo. I realized that I too was judging her and making assumptions based on her faith from my own unresolved pain and experiences.

As Sue shared how difficult this was for her, she radiated love, compassion, and raw emotion; there was no judgement or

---

[2] "Leadership Training," *Co-Active Training Institute*: https://coactive.com/training/leadership-training/.

defensiveness as you might expect from such a request. It was one of the greatest moments of leadership in all four retreats. At that moment I thought to myself, "She is a true follower of Jesus. If there are Christians like Sue, perhaps I could regain my faith." As Sue and I began our friendship, I continued my journey of faith rediscovery. Throughout it all, Sue never expressed condemnation for my very "unchristian" choices nor pressured me to return to God. Her steadfast compassion, practical advice, and friendship played a vital role in gradually guiding me to trust in God's love.

New beginnings

When I was twenty-nine, I moved to Boulder, Colorado. Over the next two years, as I worked my way out of depression, I explored all kinds of avenues for fulfillment: I worked as a consultant, I became involved in area start-up groups, and I became connected with people in a way I never had before. It was a time of forging relationships, exploring truths, working through my wounding with the help of therapists, and settling into entrepreneurship. However, I still had not found anything that satisfied the way an intimate relationship with God can.

Then, I attended a TEDx Talk event in town.[3] The event had finished, and the 3,000 attendees were streaming out of Mackie Auditorium when I looked across the stairs and saw my now-husband, Scott, a complete stranger at the time.

I had a strong premonition that this man would become an important part of my spiritual journey. I experience a premonition as an overwhelming sense that something is true or important in both the

---

[3] TEDx Talks are local speakers presenting to local audiences about everything from politics to pollination. To view talks see: https://www.ted.com/watch/tedx-talks.

physical and spiritual realm. It's stronger than intuition, and it may even be the voice of the Holy Spirit. I experience intuition daily, but this was different. It has only happened a few times in my life. It's such an intense experience that I have always heeded this voice without hesitation. And that is precisely what I did that day.

I went up to the man, shared my revelation, and asked him to read the Scriptures with me, something I hadn't done in seven years. I was shocked at what was coming out of my mouth—I hadn't even introduced myself or asked his name! Little did I know that we would be married nine months later, on July 14, 2012. Our union began a totally new spiritual phase of my life. I was terrified at first and did my best to scare him away, but the minute we became engaged, I was committed to our life together and ready to renew my faith in God. I was still wary of formal religion, so we baptized each other in the ocean and dedicated our lives and relationship to following the will of God on our own. This led me to acquire the courage and security to begin my journey as a spiritual entrepreneur—by starting Indigo Education Company.[4]

Founding Indigo

Less than a year after marrying Scott, I founded Indigo with the mission to empower the innate gifts already existing within each individual.[5] By that time, I had attended many coaching trainings and was working as a leadership coach. The idea for Indigo came to me while flying home from an executive coaching session in San Francisco. The executive I was working with told me he was a "crusty

---

[4] "Home Page," *Indigo Education Company*: https://www.indigoeducationcompany.com/.

[5] The original name of Indigo was Intrinsic Genius Technologies, followed by a brief time being called Watershed. We settled on the name Indigo in 2014 and it stuck.

old sponge" and couldn't absorb any more self-development but that his fifteen-year-old daughter would really love and value my perspective. He suggested I work with youth.

His comment struck a nerve because of my own pain growing up not knowing my value or who I really was, apart from my grades or my appearance. It occurred to me that while schools were spending inordinate amounts of time and money measuring academic "learning," they spent very little time getting to know the "learner." *Who is this unique creation and what gifts do they bring to the world?* I find that this question almost never gets asked.

In education's efforts to achieve a common external goal (a goal that has very little value in and of itself), we force kids into a programmatic box, devalue their diversity, and provide a framework for their own belief in themselves that is inherently incorrect. While systemically damaging students' sense of self, education imposes a form of measurement based on test scores and grades, which, in essence, measure the wrong thing.

I knew I wanted to shift the mindset in education from a focus on grades to a focus on the learner, but I didn't really know how. Because I had extensive experience using assessment technologies, I began with the following premise: if you measure aspects of the learner that have more value than grades, you can catalyze meaningful conversations and find powerful perspectives that instigate growth.

Based on this premise, we started the company with two basic products:

1. A comprehensive assessment that takes forty-five minutes to complete online. The assessment measures strengths, behaviors, motivators, soft skills, and social emotional

perceptions. This version of our assessment was developed in partnership with global assessment provider Target Training International (TTI) Success Insights.[6]

2. Student and teacher workshops to debrief the assessment data and build self-awareness, empathy, and freedom (our company core values).

For the first few years we went into every educational setting you can imagine across the country: large and small schools, urban and rural, rich and poor, charter and traditional, vocational and private. You name the type of school or the demographic of student, and we probably tested our product there. Based on user feedback we built a host of other products—an AI dashboard, online courses, books, curriculum, more workshops, etc. The whole process was a fascinating and eye-opening experience.

It turns out that you *can* powerfully shift mindsets by changing the nature of the measurement and conversation. I've witnessed countless transformative shifts in students, teachers, administrators and professors. Teachers in particular are hungry for a new way of valuing and seeing students. They go into education because they deeply care about making a difference. Teachers know in their hearts every single one of their students is brilliant and created for a purpose.

However, our experience also revealed just how entrenched the old factory system of education really is and how unbelievably difficult it is to alter the overall processes and measures. Far too many excellent educators leave the system because they find it difficult to follow their heart and to feel whole in the existing system. This is one of the

---

[6] "TTI Success Makes Behavioral Assessments That Reveal Human Potential`111," *TTI Success Insights*: https://www.ttisi.com/.

leading reasons we have a teacher shortage in this country. It is not pay (and our data support this).

Conclusion: How Indigo Became the Impetus for this Book

"I know that the experiences of our lives, when we let God use them, become the mysterious and perfect preparation for the work he will give us to do."[7] I couldn't agree more with the inspirational Corrie ten Boom, who wrote this quote after spending years in a concentration camp. While not as dramatic, looking back on my life, I see God using every experience as a learning tool. Moreover, the lessons I learned from my Indigo work and the reflections I'm sharing as a spiritual entrepreneur are largely intertwined:

- Just as Indigo strives to foster a different way of valuing and seeing students, this book explores different ways of valuing and understanding businesses.

- As Indigo's core values emphasize that learning must be built on a foundation of self-awareness, empathy, and freedom, so does my learning as a spiritual entrepreneur.

- Indigo is built on the premise that education is not just for "kids." We never stop learning. Life-long learning is the future of humanity. It always has been, whether or not we were conscious of it. The idea that education is something we do "to kids" rather than "with kids" is misguided. It's a co-created

---

[7] Corrie ten Boom, Elizabeth Sherrill and John Sherrill, *The Hiding Place*, 35th ed. (Grand Rapids: Chosen Books, 2006), 31.

process.[8] The same holds true for the journey of the spiritual entrepreneur: it is a continual process of growth that is co-created with the creator of the universe.

- Indigo believes a human-centered approach to education produces outcomes that are inclusive of all students and creates better outcomes for our entire society. Likewise, a human-centered approach to business that is inclusive of the *soul* will produce better outcomes for all.

The next chapter describes my experiences with spiritual entrepreneurship and how this lens can completely transform the way we view ourselves as founders, the way we see our employees, and our perspective on our companies.

---

[8] I discuss more about co-creation in the mentorship section of chapter 5.

Chapter 2

The Three Dimensions of Spiritual Entrepreneurship

When I first heard the term spiritual entrepreneurship, my heart burst with joy. They say when you put language to something, it creates meaning. Language creates the ability for someone to communicate and explore an idea more fully in a way that is not possible without language. As a new model of business, spiritual entrepreneurship requires a completely new language and mindset.[1] Knowing and exploring the language was my first step in experiencing and embodying who I am as an entrepreneur.

My Evolving Entrepreneurial Journey

Every time I've been exposed to any type of entrepreneurship, it has been a moment of personal revelation. This chapter begins with a short story of how I learned about the different types of entrepreneurs. A detailed description of spiritual entrepreneurship and my experience of its three dimensions follows.

---

[1] Spiritual entrepreneurs have existed for thousands of years, so it's not exactly a "new" model. However, formal dialogue around the concept is recent.

Entrepreneurship

Despite having a college education, I didn't really know what an entrepreneur was until my mid-twenties. Recently divorced and living in Vail, Colorado, I needed a work change and felt compelled to visit a restaurant I had never been to before. In 2004, I sat down at the bar and the man sitting next to me asked me if I needed a job. To me, it was a sign, and I began working for him shortly after.

He was the first person that embodied the role of entrepreneur to me. He came from a family of entrepreneurs who'd built a huge metals business by taking care of their employees and building innovative distribution models. He was now starting his own company and I got to experience the firsthand thrill of being in a start-up. This brilliant man loved finding new sources of high-quality metal then selling it at better prices than anyone else, creating a win-win for everyone involved. He wasn't afraid to make mistakes or take risks. He enjoyed employing people and finding new partners. When I think of entrepreneurship at its best, this man comes to mind.

After working with him for a year, I realized that I, too, was an entrepreneur, significantly changing my self-view and perspective on what was possible in life. At this point, I'd never had any formal education on the topic or read any books on entrepreneurship. Therefore, my experiential education with this dear man was a great blessing and gift, showing me that entrepreneurship in all its forms can benefit others and our world.

Social entrepreneurship

Just five years later, now living in Boulder, I resumed working part-time for that same entrepreneur while doing contract coaching and consulting. I attended many local start-up events and went to the very first public event of the Unreasonable Institute.[2] The Institute was founded by three young men who were college students at CU Boulder, and they used the phrase "social entrepreneur." I remember crying at that meeting while listening to the stories of the social entrepreneurs from around the world. It was amazing to know these people existed! I was so inspired by their stories, such as the one of a company called Greenlight Planet (now Sun King) that manufactures solar-powered lanterns and sells them at affordable prices so that people in developing nations can have easier access to power.

This was the first time that I had a concrete understanding that business owners could make money and do *good* at the same time. I became aware of the huge number of people all over the world who were successful in doing amazing things for humanity. My exposure to the Unreasonable entrepreneurs significantly contributed to the foundation of Indigo.

In my journey with Indigo, however, I realized that while social entrepreneurship is a growing field, today's investment protocols make it difficult for true social entrepreneurs to exist at scale. Even though impact investors claim they care about people over profit, the sad truth is that, in many cases, structurally—in terms of what is measured and that which gauges success—profit still matters more than people. Having social impact *without* sacrificing any profit is generally the game. I'm simply pointing out that profit still has too high of a value in the impact-investing world given the rhetoric to the contrary. This realization was painful for me as I struggled to develop Indigo while maintaining my social impact ideals. I know it is painful

---

[2] The Unreasonable Institute is now called Uncharted: https://uncharted.org/.

for many social entrepreneurs who are trying to put people before profits.

The core issue is that while social entrepreneurship was a huge step in the right direction for expanding the definition of business, the existing structures and mainstream definitions of value made it difficult for social entrepreneurship to emerge as a truly differentiated model. Moreover, social entrepreneurship doesn't leave explicit space for the soul—*the* critical part of our true existence, the eternal part of us, the part that is from God and connects back to God. Even if a social entrepreneur desires to maintain this soul connection within their company, the focus for dollar-based "return on investment" (ROI) supersedes "soul values" in the investment space almost every time.[3]

Spiritual entrepreneurship

Over a decade after my encounter with the Unreasonable Institute, when I learned about social entrepreneurship, I heard the term "spiritual entrepreneur" at our new church. Despite faith being the central theme of our marriage, Scott and I hadn't been able to find a church we both really liked. We had recently been introduced to the writings of eighteenth-century scientist and Christian mystic Emanuel Swedenborg.[4] The writings of Swedenborg were like a breath of fresh air to me. I agree with Helen Keller when she describes how it felt to read Swedenborg for the first time:

---

[3] Return on investment (ROI) is a performance measure used to evaluate the efficiency or profitability of an investment or compare the efficiency of a number of different investments: Jason Fernando, "Return on Investment (ROI): How to Calculate It and What It Means," *Investopedia,* updated on June 30, 2022, https://www.investopedia.com/terms/r/returnoninvestment.asp.

[4] Friends recommended a book called *The Presence of Other Worlds* by Wilson Van Dusen. It is one of the most accessible works on Swedenborg. Also note that Staff Chaplain James Barry, quoted previously, is a Swedenborgian pastor.

> As I realized the meaning of what I read, my soul seemed to expand and gain confidence amid the difficulties which beset me. The descriptions of the other world bore me far, far over measureless regions bathed in superhuman beauty…where great lives and creative minds cast a splendor upon darkest circumstances…where the night is lit to eternal day by the Smile of God.[5]

Scott and I were fascinated by Swedenborg's encounters with the spiritual realm and wanted to learn more. While discussing Swedenborg with another couple, we were amazed to hear that there were Swedenborgian churches. They personally knew Rich Tafel, the pastor of the Church of the Holy City in Washington, DC, and introduced us to him. COVID became an unexpected miracle in this whole situation because it enabled us to attend and join the church via Zoom.

Rich has been involved with social change in the political sphere for decades and has always had a vision that the Church of the Holy City would become a Center for Spiritual Entrepreneurship.[6] He believes that spiritual entrepreneurism offers a way to help people develop both their inner and outer lives. Many places teach you how to develop a spiritual life. Many programs teach you how to create a business or launch a political campaign. But Rich found the integration of the two in a "spiritual entrepreneur cohort" offered a new way to combine the best of free enterprise and the social sector with the goal of sustainable systemic change worldwide.

The idea of spiritual entrepreneurship suddenly made my life make sense, especially my tumultuous experiences leading Indigo. I realized that the rules of engagement for spiritual entrepreneurs were vastly

---

[5] Hellen Keller, *My Religion*, (New York: Swedenborg Foundation, 1974), 36.

[6] "Spiritual Growth, Dialogue and Community," *Church of the Holy City*: https://holycitydc.org/.

different from those of regular entrepreneurs or even social entrepreneurs—although many social entrepreneurs are actually spiritual entrepreneurs without the words to describe it, as I was. Many of us who once identified as social entrepreneurs will quickly move to the spiritual model because it is a more holistic fit: it allows space for the soul.

The Three Dimensions of Spiritual Entrepreneurship

As I mentioned in the introduction, it's very difficult to define spiritual entrepreneurship with existing language. I googled definitions on the internet, and a lot of them are good. They all have slightly different perspectives on the idea. I also looked up "spiritual" and "entrepreneur" in the dictionary.

Oxford dictionary definitions of both words are as follows:

- Spiritual: "Relating to or affecting the human spirit or soul as opposed to material or physical things"[7]

- Entrepreneur: "A person who organizes and operates a business or businesses, taking on greater than normal financial risks in order to do so"[8]

To simplify things, I settled on the following words: **Someone who runs an enterprise with the purpose of expanding love, not extracting gain.**

---

[7] Google's English Dictionary, provided by Oxford Languages, s.v. "define spiritual," Google search.
[8] Google's English Dictionary, provided by Oxford Languages, s.v. "define entrepreneur," Google search.

I replaced the word business with enterprise because it's more inclusive. Many people tend to think of business owners as limited to people who start for-profit companies. People who found non-profits, sole-ownership businesses, and part-time entities as well as gig-workers, such as independent contractors and freelancers, are all *business owners* from this inclusive definition. "Greater than normal financial risks" is not directly included as part of the definition. However, that is still true, possibly even more so, for those starting a spiritual enterprise versus a typical business.

There is an inherent tension within spiritual entrepreneurship of having to deliver material products or services while maintaining a focus on non-material aspects of humanity. Ultimately, the movement behind spiritual entrepreneurship is a redefinition of what is valuable—a new and more meaningful return on investment, so to speak. A spiritual entrepreneur values the people, or the intrinsic, as most important, whereas, generally, our society values the money, or the extrinsic, as most important. Our government and public institutions value organization and structure, or the systemic, as most important.[9]

Moreover, the valuation of a spiritual enterprise goes far beyond our very limited perspective as humans locked into our time and space continuum. A spiritual enterprise attempts to pursue an eternal perspective in which there is a benevolent Creator, or God, who loves all of us and is intimately involved in the unfolding human story. From God's perspective, there are an infinite number of dimensions of impact, defined as any positive change in the physical, spiritual, or emotional growth of humans, our planet, and beyond! Most of these

---

[9] Intrinsic, extrinsic, and systemic are concepts from Dr. Robert S. Hartman and are defined in detail in chapter 4.

impacts are not numerically measurable, but you wouldn't want to measure them even if you could.

The very nature of spiritual journeys is that they are unique, and their most important aspects are often largely indescribable via language. Because of this, I in no way want to limit the exploration of this field by putting labels or structure around something that is so organic and personal. However, because putting language to something is critical to expanding the conversation, I want to share three core dimensions of spiritual entrepreneurship that have importance to me.

1. **Founder focus**, the first dimension: The business is an integral part of the founder's spiritual journey.

2. **Employee focus**, the second dimension: Employees who work for the spiritual enterprise, whether they know it or not, encounter the company because it's part of their spiritual path.

3. **Business focus**, the third dimension: The business itself has a life force of its own, and the purpose of that business is to help humanity evolve into a higher level of consciousness and/or to reveal the kingdom of heaven on earth (these essentially mean the same thing in my mind).

These three dimensions of spiritual entrepreneurship happen simultaneously and work together to produce the greatest possible result. However, as a founder, it can feel confusing and challenging to juggle these three dimensions while also trying to start, manage, and run a business.

Founder focus, the first dimension: the spiritual entrepreneur's personal journey

All souls come to earth for spiritual growth. The process of becoming human and grappling with what it means to be human is important on a much larger plane than we realize, so much so that God himself went through the process in the form of Jesus Christ. Franciscan friar Father Richard Rohr describes this process: "We are spiritual beings trying to learn to be human, not the other way around."[10]

Christin Myrick, one of my very dearest friends, can see souls—she experiences the seeing as an imprint or an expression of someone's deepest and truest self. As each physical person is unique, each soul is unique. Christin finds there to be "types" of souls that work together in an ecosystem, much like in nature. Each soul's type and form provides a glimpse into their divine purpose.

Here is how Christin describes divine purpose in her book *Your Fearless Soul*:

> Everything has a place and a purpose, including you. Your divine purpose is [a] meaningful contribution that only you can make. It is the way you belong to the world: your unique way of being for a long period of time.
>
> Your divine purpose is deeper than a skill set or a talent, deeper than personality or persona. Your divine purpose is not something you have to do...[It] aligns with the most essential part of you who you are on the level of Soul. Divine purpose flows through you... To

---

[10] This quote can be found in many Rohr articles, such as Richard Rohr, "Fully Human," May 16, 2016, *Center for Action and Contemplation*: https://cac.org/fully-human-2016-05-16/.

choose and claim your divine purpose is to have a truly Fearless Soul.[11]

When Christin first saw my soul, I appeared to her as a Queen who had the ability to bless or curse people, a conqueror of sorts who is meant to go out and win people's hearts and minds. The critical point she made was that my job was to reveal and build *the* kingdom, not *my* kingdom. This idea of growing the kingdom of heaven is central to the spiritual entrepreneur conversation. It must not be about you and your work. It is about collectively contributing to and revealing the kingdom of heaven that already exists.

You must decide on which kingdom—yours or God's—you'd like to see emerge and how your venture contributes to that. Whether you interpret Jesus's words in Luke 17:21 as having the kingdom of heaven "within you" or "among you," the impact is the same, and you must seek it, discover it, and choose it for yourself.

It's interesting how people seem to recognize their spiritual side on different levels and at various places. Choosing to embrace the journey or run away from it impacts our destiny after we transition back into the spiritual realm. It is my observation through working with young people that more and more youth have come to earth instinctively knowing and embracing this destiny. When they look around at the world's systems, they can feel depressed and even suicidal because there aren't many good examples in mainstream society of how to live life as if you were indeed a spiritual being on a purpose-driven journey.

---

[11] Christin Myrick, *Your Fearless Soul* (Birdhouse Publishing LLC, 2015).

The role of fear and resistance

It's sad to me that so many people don't choose the spiritual path because of fear and self-doubt when, in fact, these emotions are indicators that they are probably moving in the right direction. There is a reason why almost every encounter with an angel in the Bible begins with the phrase, "Do not be afraid." Fear is natural in the process.

One of the most profound books on this topic is *The War of Art* by Steven Pressfield. As a writer, he describes purpose through the lens of an artist, but it's very similar to that of a spiritual entrepreneur. The antagonist in the book is Resistance and how it stops us from doing our soul work. Below are quotes from the book:

> Fear is good. Like self-doubt, fear is an indicator. Fear tells us what we have to do.
>
> Remember our rule of thumb: The more scared we are of a work or calling, the more sure we can be that we have to do it.
>
> Resistance is experienced as fear; the degree of fear equates to the strength of Resistance. Therefore, the more fear we feel about a specific enterprise, the more certain we can be that that enterprise is important to us and to the growth of our soul. That's why we feel so much Resistance. If it meant nothing to us, there'd be no Resistance.[12]

When somebody feels that an enterprise is a part of their spiritual path, they may be terrified. The founding, growing, and tending of the enterprise is a critical part of a business owner's growth journey, and

---

[12] Steven Pressfield, *The War of Art: Break Through the Blocks and Win Your Inner Creative Battles* (New York: Black Irish Entertainment, 2012), 40.

it's a daunting undertaking. The spiritual entrepreneur may not have it all figured out and will not necessarily have a personal track record of success. Instead, it is more likely to be the opposite. It is far more likely that this person will lack self-confidence, plagued with resistance and struggle.

While fear on your journey is common, it's essential to understand the difference between natural fear when stepping into our divine purpose and fear that separates us from our true selves, others, and God. I liken the journey of the spiritual entrepreneur to the Israelites wandering around the desert. So often, fear pulled them away from God and their destiny, causing devastating consequences. One poignant example of this is the golden calf of Exodus 32.

Rabbi David Fohrman talks about the golden calf incident from the perspective of fear versus awe. He describes how the people imagined that Moses was dead on the mountain and decided that building and worshiping a golden calf was safer than knowing God. In their fearful response, they missed the truth of who they were—God's beloved children, and who God is—the benevolent creator of the universe. When you know these two things, fear changes to awe. And awe brings us closer to truth and union. "With awe, I don't want to hide or pull away. I want to come closer," Rabbi Fohrman says.[13]

This is why self-development is vital to the spiritual entrepreneur, and I dedicate a whole chapter to it. We must develop a strong sense of ourselves and who God is, which takes time.

---

[13] Rabbi David Forhman, "Yamim Noraim: Meaning & Significance," *Aleph Beta Recording*, video, https://www.alephbeta.org/playlist/yamim-noraim-confusing-satan.

Your journey is not just about you

God led the Israelites for forty years to get to their destination. If theirs were simply a physical journey, they could have arrived in just a few months. Entering the Promised Land was not the only point of their journey: many lessons were learned along the way. The next generation reached the Promised Land after the first generation all died (Numbers 32:13). It's like that in terms of the kingdom of heaven: we're all building something for someone else, not ourselves.

For the past ten years, I've felt like I was wandering the desert. To many observers, Indigo's journey would have seemed aimless. I'm sure they couldn't understand why, with the goal seemingly so close, we couldn't "cross over" the line of success. But as I mentioned above, wandering serves its own divine purpose and helps to catalyze much learning. The journey of a spiritual entrepreneur is much more important than the goal. As with the Israelites in the desert, it is even possible that a spiritual entrepreneur's job may be to simply lay the groundwork for the next generation. Their goal may never be achieved in their own lifetime.[14] These sacrificial efforts are essential: many before us have laid the groundwork that has directly allowed humanity to realize and acknowledge our current state of advancement.

The impact of the Israelites' journey cannot be underestimated—following God's pillar of fire, eating the manna every day, watching everyone who remembered the old way of slavery die. Simple daily practices were critical so that when the Israelites did inherit the Promised Land, they could do something good with it. Similarly, the impact of the journey, and what is learned during it, should not be disregarded for a spiritual entrepreneur: often it is what is learned, or

---

[14] Many of the Jewish patriarchs and early Christians shared this perspective: "These were all commended for their faith, yet none of them received what had been promised" (Hebrews 11:39).

the maturity gained, during that period that allows something good to be done through the spiritual venture.

The idea that we are all on a spiritual journey is hardly new. Homer's *Iliad* spoke to fate and free will over a thousand years ago. More recently we have Joseph Campbell's *The Hero's Journey*, Paulo Coelho's *The Pilgrimage* and *The Alchemist*, Bill Plotkin's *Nature and the Human Soul*, and so many more. These models have been useful to me and can be useful to other spiritual entrepreneurs. However, I've felt as if they don't quite capture all the elements involved when you're combining the spiritual journey with business.

Employee focus, the second dimension: the work is part of your employees' spiritual path

The corporate world is slowly moving toward an employee-first culture. This idea has existed for a very long time but is now regaining traction. During the Great Depression, W.K. Kellogg decided to add a fourth shift to his factory, adding 30% more jobs to help unemployed people in the city. This provided all his employees a six-hour workday versus the previous eight-hour shifts. By the second year of doing this, all employees were making the same amount of money they made working eight hours, and productivity increased overall. When the US Department of Labor interviewed workers, *freedom* was the word most used when describing the impact of their new schedule. Many workers also described the positive effects of a six-hour workday on their family and community.[15]

---

[15] Wayne Muller, *Sabbath: Finding Rest, Renewal, and Delight in Our Busy Lives* (Bantam Books, 1999), 103-106.

This example is profound because working less actually benefitted everyone involved. Freedom of the worker became prioritized over consumerism, and technological productivity gains were shared by everyone in the system for the greater good not just the benefit of the corporate shareholders.

Today, many companies like Patagonia, IBM, Southwest, Gore-TEX, and Starbucks also strive to put employees first, but I've never seen anything quite like what Mr. Kellogg did almost one hundred years ago! It's a shame that the six-hour shift at Kellogg was permanently reversed in 1984; the grand experiment was over and largely forgotten in corporate America. The fact that most manufacturing plants now operate with two twelve-hour shifts is a sad reminder that we've forgotten that less can be more.[16]

It's difficult for public companies, even registered B Corporations that meet high standards of balancing purpose and profit, to implement people first in the purest sense.[17] They are still beholden to the structure of Wall Street, where climbing profits are needed to keep shareholders happy and the focus is more on short-term results than long-term benefits.

The spiritual entrepreneur takes this idea of "employee first" and moves it into yet another dimension. In this model, not only are people first, but the team members who have been attracted to an organization are participating because it's part of *their* spiritual path. This idea has completely changed the way I think about my employees. The word

---

[16] I'm advocating for more choice here rather than saying that twelve-hour shifts are universally bad; I know some people who prefer them to have four days off.

[17] Certified B Corporations are a new kind of business that balances purpose and profit. They are legally required to consider the impact of their decisions on their workers, customers, suppliers, community, and the environment, not just shareholders: "Measuring a company's entire social and environmental impact," About B Corp Certification, *B Corporation*: https://bcorporation.net/.

"employee" has never felt quite right to me. As I consider the concept of "people first" in spiritual entrepreneurship, I wonder if that is what Jesus meant when he said, "I have called you friends" (John 15:15). A hierarchical relationship didn't really work for Jesus. It doesn't work for me either: if you are journeying together toward goals that are bigger than both of you, "friend," or "team member," rather than "employee," seems to be a more apt description of the relationship.

The irony of being a spiritually minded CEO is that you are the leader: you hold the vision, yet you hardly know where you are headed. Rather, you hold space for the journey to have a higher purpose and keep people focused on the company's agreed-upon mission.[18] The idea of a career arc, or all the peaks and valleys of your journey, takes on a whole new meaning when viewed from this wider lens. Work can be one of the most profound vehicles for spiritual development if one lets it be.

Holding the belief that your employees are engaged in the company for spiritual growth sounds noble in theory, but I find the practice of actually *doing* it challenging. At the end of the day, a business owner still needs employees to get their work done, be engaged, and take personal responsibility. In other words, working from a spiritual perspective doesn't mean that you don't have to express the expectations and needs of the company, or that you won't feel frustrated at times. It just means those aspects are less important than the human soul who happens to work for you in this moment.

For example, when I'm interviewing, I try to have a conversation rather than go through a formulaic process. This is mainly because of my personal trauma with interviews. They feel so false. I often feel

---

[18] Holding space is a coaching term that means being physically, emotionally and mentally present for someone to move through their own process of transformation.

evaluated as an object rather than as a human. As a result, I've failed every formal interview I've ever participated in by getting sweaty, going blank mentally, and almost passing out. The goal of interviews at Indigo is to see if that spark of connection is present and if there is a real desire to do the job. If so, we start working together on a contract-to-hire basis to see if the fit is there. It's always obvious within two months if it's going to work out, and I trust that whatever happens is okay. When people decide to move on, it's also okay. They are moving in a different direction on *their* journey, and I attempt to support that transition in whatever way I can.

The spiritual purpose of why someone is drawn to Indigo is often not obvious. It's also important that I don't become wrapped up in thinking that I know what the purpose is because often I've been wrong. Moreover, many employees don't see themselves as being on a spiritual journey, especially at work. The main point for me as a spiritual entrepreneur is to not impose my will or beliefs on someone who works for me but rather to hold *myself* to a higher standard of care and perspective. I hardly ever talk to my employees about God unless they specifically bring it up. I simply try to elevate the conversation to something more meaningful whenever I can.

For example, if someone isn't getting a specific task done, I don't think they are lazy or purposely not doing the task. Instead, I've learned that it usually means there is some sort of block to the task that is tied to something deeper in their life. Often, it's connected to childhood trauma. If our relationship is close, I can talk about it directly with them, and we have profound conversations. The conversation may or may not solve the problem, but it always deescalates the situation and presents a new way forward. If our relationship is not close enough to warrant that type of direct depth, I ask questions differently to gain a new perspective for them and myself so we can navigate task execution in a more human way.

It's exhausting trying to keep my mind on the tasks and the structure of the day-to-day along with the deeper meaning of things. I still struggle with everything business owners struggle with: salaries, time off, meeting structure, accountability, planning, and teams. I feel guilty because we've never had enough cash flow to pay people market rates and so I often wonder if they know how valuable they are. I often hold my breath waiting for them to leave because I know they can get higher-paying jobs elsewhere.

As a business owner managing a handful of people, the list of details that causes me stress goes on and on. I often judge myself as not good enough for the job. I all too easily believe the voices that tell me I'm the problem, that I'm just not cut out for managing people, and if I were a better leader, I wouldn't worry so much. I wish I could say I've moved past these struggles, but as I said before, I'm in the middle of this exploration of spiritual entrepreneurship, and I'm constantly making progress and experiencing setbacks simultaneously.

In many ways, I am still in the midst of my wandering journey rather than right around the corner from the Promised Land, and I'm learning this is okay. I know the journey serves its purpose, even if I can't see it yet. I've found that when I take time to reflect, new strategies present themselves just in time. The "Tools for the Trade" chapter in this book describe many of the strategies that have been helpful to me thus far.

Business focus, the third dimension: the business itself exists for the purpose of elevating human consciousness in some way

"Elevating human consciousness" sounds rather daunting and may put people off from wanting to start a spiritual enterprise, but it isn't as complicated as it may sound. I see humanity naturally evolving to a place of unity. That may seem hard to imagine based on all the turmoil, but when you take a step back and look at how much the world has progressed overall in the past two thousand years, the change is remarkable.

Our technology is beyond the scope of the imagination of people even one hundred years ago. Medical and scientific advancements are emerging daily. Globally, people care about the planet and animals at an unprecedented level. While we have not achieved equality, more and more people are inclusive of all of humanity regardless of gender, sexual orientation, or skin color. Our progress is uneven, and messy, but this is all part of the "imprecise human journey."

Elevating human consciousness is synonymous with revealing the kingdom of heaven. Humanity's positive changes are moving us in the direction of the kingdom of heaven that Jesus described. This kingdom does not arrive through military campaigns or violence toward evil—as Jesus's disciples thought—but by individual acts of expanding love. Journalist Michael Gerson shares his perspective on this process, considering the current nationalism movement in America:

God's kingdom would grow silently, soul by soul, "among you" and "within you," across every barrier of nation or race — in acts of justice, peacemaking, love, inclusion, meekness, humility, and gentleness.[19]

Spiritual enterprises have missions to grow the kingdom of heaven by expanding love, thus growing heavenly qualities. We can choose to play a part in that kingdom or not, but it's emerging all the same. Therefore, if you identify as a spiritual entrepreneur and are wondering if your business idea elevates human consciousness or helps reveal the kingdom of heaven, you need only look to your own heart to know if that is true. Impacting the spiritual makeup of humanity can be as simple as changing the lives of a few kids or running your solo business in a way that increases love and forgiveness in the world.

Several people I see regularly for professional services, such as my hair stylist, physical trainer, and therapist, run their businesses in a way that feels full of love. Think about small coffee shops you've gone into where the employees personally know their customers and the community is better simply because of their existence. Our hearts matter: it's very difficult to judge if a business is elevating human consciousness simply by looking at its outward appearance.

> But the Lord said to Samuel, "Do not look on his appearance or on the height of his stature, because I have rejected him. For the Lord sees not as man sees: man looks on the outward appearance, but the Lord looks on the heart." (1 Samuel 16:7)

---

[19] Michael Gerson, "Opinion: Trump should fill Christians with rage. How come he doesn't," *The Washington Post*, September 01, 2022, https://www.washingtonpost.com/opinions/2022/09/01/michael-gerson-evangelical-christian-maga-democracy/.

Based on the previous Scripture, I would suggest that we should not be quick to assume that a company that looks good and communicates all the right things is doing good. Even God's great prophet Samuel was taken by Saul's physical appearance and didn't immediately recognize David as God's chosen king.

On the flip side, we must be careful not to overlook those who might not look like they are doing anything because their worth may be immeasurably more than we can imagine.

Organizational development models

Thought leaders have been exploring the role of the business entity in shifting human consciousness for decades. As a result, there are several emerging models for evolved company management.

Well-known models for organizational development are Ken Wilbur's integral theory and Don Beck's spiral dynamics.[20] From a business perspective, I find vertical development to be a useful model to translate those ideas into workplace behaviors.[21] The following chart, created by Frederic Laloux, describes each of the stages of development and what they mean in terms of human collaboration.

---

[20] For more information, see Frederic Laloux, *Reinventing Organizations: A Guide to Creating Organizations Inspired by the Next Stage in Human Consciousness*, Foreword by Ken Wilber, (Nelson Parker, 2014), https://www.reinventingorganizations.com/
"Integral theory (Ken Wilber)," *Wikipedia*, last modified November 22, 2022, https://en.m.wikipedia.org/wiki/Integral_theory_(Ken_Wilber) and "Spiral Dynamics," *Wikipedia*, last modified June 16, 2022, 16:30, https://en.m.wikipedia.org/wiki/Spiral_Dynamics.

[21] Dede Henley, "Research Says Vertical Development Can Make You a Better Leader," *Forbes*, January 31, 2020, https://www.forbes.com/sites/.
"Developing Talent? You're probably Missing Vertical Development," Leading Effectively Article, *Center for Creative Leadership*, www.ccl.org/articles/.

Evolutionary Breakthroughs in Human Collaboration

Color	Description	Guiding Metaphor	Key Breakthroughs	Current Examples
RED	Constant exercise of power by chief to keep foot soldiers in line. Highly reactive, short-term focus. Thrives in chaotic environments.	Wolf pack	· Division of labor · Command authority	· Organized crime · Street gangs · Tribal militias
AMBER	Highly formal roles within a hierarchical pyramid. Top-down command and control. Future is repetition of the past.	Army	· Formal roles (stable and scalable hierarchies) · Stable, replicable processes (long-term perspectives)	· Catholic Church · Military · Most government organizations (public school systems, police departments)
ORANGE	Goal is to beat competition; achieve profit and growth. Management by objectives (command and control over what, freedom over how).	Machine	· Innovation · Accountability · Meritocracy	· Multinational companies · Investment banks · Charter schools
GREEN	Focus on culture and empowerment to boost employee motivation. Stakeholders replace shareholders as primary purpose.	Family	· Empowerment · Egalitarian management · Stakeholder model	Businesses known for idealistic practices (Ben & Jerry's, Southwest Airlines, Starbucks, Zappos)
TEAL	Self-management replaces hierarchical pyramid. Organizations are seen as living entities, oriented toward realizing their potential.	Living organism	· Self-management · Wholeness · Evolutionary purpose	Possibly some few pioneering organizations

Source: The Future of Management is Teal by Frederic Laloux

Today, the organizations where we have the greatest labor shortages tend to be the ones where there are a lot of Amber/Army attributes, as described in the second row in the chart above. This approach to life does not work well with most people anymore, and it disempowers people who want to make a difference and drive innovation.

For example, a significant number of purpose-driven educators I've known over the past ten years have left education because they feel the school system has killed their soul in a way that leaves them feeling hopeless and powerless. The same is true for many people in the healthcare system, who want to heal people but become trapped in a system that dehumanizes them and destroys their spirit. People who operate at the Green and Teal levels of consciousness in the chart find it excruciating to work in Amber organizations.

Because Amber organizations think about human capital in outdated ways, the salaries they offer are not high enough to attract and retain top talent. The fact that as teachers grow in seniority they will never make as much as administrators, despite having the more impactful and challenging jobs, demonstrates this unfortunate side effect of Amber thinking.

Most of our modern, commercial companies are still in the Orange/Machine stage of development. These companies are still able to attract talent due to their profit and innovation focus. However, many employees of these companies also end up feeling disengaged and disillusioned due to feeling a lack of connection and value as an individual. The pandemic accelerated these feelings of unrest as people took time to examine the level of meaning in their lives.

Green/Family companies tend to have an easier time attracting and retaining top talent because their human collaboration practices are more aligned with our current collective level of consciousness. Supporting companies in shifting into a Green way of being will result in a more productive workforce and an overall healthier population.

Teal/Living Organism organizations are beginning to emerge. While I would like to run Indigo as a Teal company, it is challenging because, as a society, we are not yet at this stage of human consciousness. The concept of a Teal organization can be a useful roadmap for how a spiritual entrepreneur aims to run their business. Laloux describes Teal companies as possessing the following characteristics:[22]

- **Self-management**: Peer relationships replace rigid hierarchical management structures. Individuals have high autonomy in their domain.

- **Wholeness**: Individuals bring their whole selves to work, not just the characteristics deemed to be professional.

- **Evolutionary purpose**: The organization has a purpose of its own and attempts to sense what the world wants. As a result, organization members are more agile, creating from circumstances rather than trying to control them.

The concept of evolutionary purpose in Teal organizations very much aligns with the spiritual entrepreneurship dimension of businesses having their own purpose. James Fischer, another thought leader in this field, would take this a step further, describing organizations as living organisms, each with its own unique growth path: "Every living thing has an ideal path of growth, including business enterprises."[23] In his book *Navigating the Growth Curve,* Fischer describes a business's stages of growth not by revenue but by the number of people an organization has. This is another example of refocusing the business conversation on the people rather than money or the product.

---

[22] Monica Giannobile, "What is a Teal Organization?" *Workology*, February 17, 2022, https://workology.com/what-is-a-teal-organization/, and Frederic Laloux, "The Future of Management is Teal," *Strategy+Business: A PWC Publication*, July 06, 2015, https://www.strategy-business.com/article/00344.

[23] James Fischer, *Navigating the Growth Curve* (Boulder: Growth Curve Press, 2006), 53.

From within the framework of Teal, leadership must be committed to the personal growth of themselves as well as each member. Leadership consultant Dr. Cybelle Lyon states that "an organization reflects the developmental stage of the majority of its leaders," and after more than two decades work in this field, she notices an encouraging shift:

> I see more and more leaders with both the desire and capability to not just lead the business, but to lead humanity in a noble direction. This gives me hope that it could be our business leaders who, replacing greed and ego with altruistic motives, will take our society in a better, more evolved direction.
>
> What will it look like if we continue this trend of more frequently demanding our business leaders show characteristics such as integrity, empathy, and purpose instead of bravado and 'strength'?[24]

If we embrace workforce goals that embody the Teal level of human collaboration, it will produce the best outcome for our employers, citizens, and communities. Approaching the future of work with a Teal lens puts the labor shortage problem into a holistic and restorative perspective. It requires retraining our own hearts and minds, which is none other than the goal of life itself.

These emerging models of organizational development hold much promise for helping spiritual entrepreneurs define their business practices and leverage research on their own paths.

---

[24] Cybelle Lyon, Email to author, 2021.

The tension of a spiritual enterprise: redefining control and success

The interesting thing about a business having a life force of its own is that you can't really control it. It seems to have its own timing. You might have a great product, hire the best people, do all the "right" things, and still find that nothing is working because the timing isn't right yet. I feel like we have very little to do with whether a true spiritual enterprise succeeds or fails in the traditional sense of those words. It will do what it's meant to do, and we are along for the ride of learning.

From this perspective, it's difficult to define "success." Like a parent who just birthed a child, you might have preconceived notions about what success looks like for the child. However, those notions can sometimes damage the child rather than support them to achieve their purpose. Your idea of success might be for your child to become a doctor, make a lot of money, find a spouse, and have two kids and a house with the white picket fence. That is all well and good, but what if your dream for their life prevents them from living *their* dream?

It's a very common theme that comes up when I coach young people. One college student had changed her major three times and was ready to drop out of school when she came to me in tears. She felt her life would be a failure if she did not pursue the science major she thought her parents wanted for her. Of course, nothing could have been further from the truth. Her parents wanted her to be happy, but she didn't know or believe that. Once we convinced her to pursue her dreams, she graduated on time and pursued a successful career as a nutritionist.

This example is a parallel to one of those paradoxes that constantly exist in the world of spiritual entrepreneurship. On one hand, you birthed the company. It came from your heart and your mind and your hard work. Therefore, it only makes sense that you should have some control over where your company goes and what success looks like. And indeed, as the CEO, you must step forth to lead each moment. You cannot abandon your post, although, believe me, I've wanted to many, many times.

On the other hand, your company isn't really yours at all: ultimately, it is God's. Therefore, you must walk a fine line of imposing your own will while surrendering your will at the same time. What you do matters, and the effort is worth it, but the company is God's. Everything is God's anyway, and a spiritual enterprise is even more so because it's about revealing divine light. God's definition of success is the only one that matters. The tricky part is that it's not easy to understand what success is in God's eyes.

I'll go back to the story of Moses because the Exodus is such a vivid example. Moses's job was to lead the people wherever God wanted, not where Moses or the people wanted. The people had a will of their own, of course. They were certainly a pain in the neck. They made so many mistakes that God felt like destroying them at least three times and Moses argued to keep them alive. You might think success in this case would have been marching right into the Promised Land and becoming rich and powerful. If that were the measure, this story was certainly not a successful one, but it did meet God's definition of success.

God's definition of success almost always includes some form of increasing love and freedom. God had delivered the Israelites from slavery in Egypt, but they were still slaves to their own thoughts, beliefs, and ways of life. One of my favorite Biblical podcasts, BEMA, puts it this way: "God got them out of Egypt, but the more challenging task was getting Egypt out of the people."²⁵ It was more important to God that the people be freed of their limiting beliefs to accept his love than it was for them to inhabit the Promised Land immediately.

The tension of a spiritual enterprise: revealing light from darkness

One of the greatest privileges of being a human on earth is the ability to reveal light from darkness. This is one measure of success for a spiritual entrepreneur and, of course, it is impossible to actually measure. One of my teachers, Vince Jordan, is a Kabbalistic Jew and a spiritual entrepreneur. He started Lobaki, a virtual reality academy for schools across the country, with a focus on youth who are most at risk. He is now working with the Optima Foundation to create the world's first virtual reality classical charter school. Vince delights in helping young people become creators with technology and revealing the light of God (whom he refers to as Havayah).²⁶ He wrote the following:

> The [Jewish] Sages say that when our neshama (souls) are in the heavenly realm, they discuss coming here because here is where we have the opportunity to release light from darkness and no such opportunity exists in the heavenly realms. We know that Havayah (God) delights more in light from darkness than in just light alone and our neshama delight in delighting Havayah!²⁷

If we believe that, then we can appreciate the darkness and the struggle it takes to reveal the light. This tension of darkness and light is

---

[25] "The BEMA Podcast," *BEMA Discipleship*: https://www.bemadiscipleship.com/.

[26] Havayah is the pronunciation used for God's essential Name spelled with the four letters י-הוה (yud, hei, vav, hei): https://www.inner.org/names/namhavay.htm.

[27] Vince Jordan, Email to author, 2021.

reflected in the constant tension of living in multiple realities, and the tension of living as both physical and spiritual beings. It is the act of working through the process of not knowing that brings about transformation, or light from the darkness. This has been my experience. In one sense, everything you do (or don't do) matters, and in another sense, you don't matter at all.

There are at least as many paths to God's kingdom as there are people, and God knows each of them intimately. It reminds me of the story of Queen Esther deciding between risking death by approaching the King to save her people or choosing to remain silent. Her uncle, Mordechai, tells Esther:

> For if you remain silent at this time, relief and deliverance for the Jews will arise from another place, but you and your father's family will perish. And who knows but that you have come to your royal position for such a time as this? (Esther 4:14)

Esther chose her path. God would have had deliverance for his people regardless of her choice, but she chose to embrace her destiny of being a part of God's plan for his kingdom. As spiritual entrepreneurs, we are invited onto one of the paths to God's kingdom to participate in the struggle to reveal light from the darkness. The tension of walking with that struggle, while also running a functioning business, means we must be flexible with our definition of success if we are to stay on the path.

Conclusion: Putting It All Together with Integrative Ability

Thus, spiritual entrepreneurs are constantly holding the three dimensions of founder, employee and business with simultaneous focus on, respectively:

1. Personal growth
2. Development of others
3. Elevation of human consciousness or, alternatively, revealing the kingdom of heaven on earth via their company's mission

They are constantly integrating these three dimensions—and the focus of each—with the realities of actually running a business. For this reason, integrative ability is one of the greatest leadership skills that spiritual founders must cultivate. Integrative ability creates a better whole by allowing for complexity, dynamic movement, uncertainty, and opposing perspectives.

The mind (and especially the ego) is not capable of handling the integrated dimensions of spiritual entrepreneurship on its own. This process takes the mind, body, heart, and soul all working together. It also requires God's grace. It's an incredibly complex dance, and yet it can be as simple as breathing if a person can get into a state of flow.

Integrating the masculine and feminine

One of the most relevant examples of integrative ability is balancing the masculine and feminine energy we all have. To understand this concept, it may be helpful to use the Chinese concepts for masculine and feminine energy, yang and yin, respectively.[28] Interestingly, wealth measured from a yang perspective may be viewed by productivity, achievement, and material things. From a yin perspective wealth may be viewed by unseen things: time, friendship, and love. Yin values of wealth cannot be quantified, counted, and boxed. They are free and wild.

The inability to quantify yin wealth is one of the key reasons societies have been so dismissive of feminine-energy contributions to society. GDP is a prime example of this: the immeasurable contributions of stay-at-home moms (and dads) and those who make time to volunteer in all aspects of their communities are in no way acknowledged or measured in a country's GDP.[29]

When you read about feminine energy, there are many similarities to the energy required in spiritual entrepreneurship: openness, connection, and flow, to name a few. I might be biased because I am a woman, but I love the way feminine energy feels and moves in relation to business and life. It feels more like a rhythm or a song to me. When I lead from the feminine, I'm less tired, more nurturing, fully alive, grounded, and connected. It doesn't mean there isn't a lot of value in understanding and leveraging masculine energy. For example, when a complex project requires highly focused attention, I may access my masculine energy to get the work done efficiently. Masculine versus feminine is not the answer: balance is the key, not favoring one or the other.

---

[28] There are many articles and books written on yin and yang. For a short one, see *Encyclopedia Britannica*, s.v., "Yin Yang," last modified August 25, 2022, https://www.britannica.com/topic/yinyang.

[29] "Why isn't household production included in the GDP?" *Bureau of Economic Analysis*, https://www.bea.gov/help/. For some interesting thoughts on GDP, see "GDP," Econlib Guides, *Library of Economics and Liberty*: https://www.econlib.org/library/Topics/College/gdp.html.

From a biblical standpoint, the idea of the feminine, though often overlooked, is also quite pronounced. While we typically reference God using masculine pronouns, God embodies both the masculine and the feminine. The very first chapter of the Bible says that God created the heavens and the earth and made both man and woman in his image. If both man and woman are made in God's image, then God encompasses all male and female qualities as well. I personally feel the presence of the Holy Spirit in a distinctly feminine way. The church being described as the "bride of Christ" would suggest that our position in relation to God is feminine. The Song of Solomon describes the relationship in vivid detail.

In Judaism, there is the idea of the divine feminine known as *shekhinah*.[30] The word is derived from the Hebrew root meaning "to dwell or settle." The shekhinah embodies the creative force at the heart of all existence. In the Bible, it's most used to refer to God's presence in the tabernacle as well as the temple in Jerusalem. From the perspective of God living within us, shekhinah is the "indwelling." Spiritual entrepreneurs awaken the shekhinah energy by seeing God in all things, thus bringing heaven to earth.

It appears there is much to learn from embracing and exploring feminine aspects of both God and business. Spiritual entrepreneurship is an aligned framework for doing so. Traditional business, and society in general, has been out of balance by favoring the masculine for too long. I've had potential investors ask me what *male* CEO I most wanted to emulate. A female CEO wasn't part of their thought schema, even though they were talking to me. As it turns out, "myself" was *not* an acceptable answer.

---

[30] Lauren Tuchman, "The Shekhinah or The Divine Presence or Divine Feminine in Judaism," *State of Formation*, January 18, 2012, https://stateofformation.org/2012/01/the-shekhinah-or-the-divine-presence-or-divine-feminine-in-judaism/.

Interestingly, there are theories that the global balance of masculine and feminine energy has already shifted, but society hasn't quite "caught up" yet. In 2011, I went to a talk given by a futurist in Colorado that struck me. The talk was about the Mayan Calendar. According to the speaker, the Mayan Calendar predicted every major epoch of humanity.[31] Apparently, it ended in 2012. Some people thought it meant the world would end, but really, she explained, it meant that the world would shift from a predominantly masculine energy to a predominantly feminine energy. If this is true, it's good news for spiritual entrepreneurs!

Balancing the masculine and feminine is just one example of how spiritual entrepreneurs must dynamically hold and integrate many perspectives. The next chapter illustrates how traditional entrepreneurship operates around a masculine-energy model of exclusivity, ranking and sorting, and money—single bottom-line return on investment. This dominant model explains why funding in the current capital system is so difficult for spiritual founders and causes much of that tension spiritual entrepreneurs face on a regular basis.

---

[31] I do not have the name of the speaker on this topic, but the talk was held at the DaVinci Institute in Louisville, CO. See https://davinciinstitute.com/about-us/.

CHAPTER 3
THE THREE PRINCIPLES OF VENTURE CAPITAL

Before Indigo was "launched," I found it quite easy to raise money from angel investors and friends.[1] I had a strong vision, there was a need in the marketplace, our pro forma was amazing, and I didn't know anything about the education system, which made me overconfident.[2] God bless my investors who decided to take the leap with me, or we wouldn't even have started. As Indigo began to take shape, however, it became more and more difficult to go through the process of pitching to capital sources. It was challenging on a surface level: as we continued to miss our revenue targets, we became less attractive as an investment. That made sense to me.

However, on a deeper level, I was taken off guard by a pain growing inside that stemmed from a lack of congruence within myself: the more investors I spoke with, the more I realized that the game they expected me to play and what I wanted in my heart were two different

---

[1] An angel investor is a high-net-worth individual who provides financial backing for entrepreneurs, typically in exchange for ownership equity in the company: Akhilesh Ganti, "Angel Investor Definition and How It Works," *Investopedia*, March 22, 2022, https://www.investopedia.com/terms/a/angelinvestor.asp.

[2] Pro forma financial statements incorporate hypothetical amounts, forecasts, or estimates, built into the data to give a "picture" of a company's profits: Alicia Tuovila, "Pro Forma: What It Means and How to Create Pro Forma Financial Statements," *Investopedia*, August 20, 2022, https://www.investopedia.com/terms/p/proforma.asp.

things. This left me feeling like I needed to present a version of myself that didn't truly reflect who I was, simply to prove my worth from a financial perspective. This affected my self-confidence and sense of personal value. It was a confusing time, especially because at that point, most of the reflections that are documented in this book had not yet fully formed in my mind.

This confusion led me to compromise my values, which was reminiscent of my time in the cult-like church. Once again, I felt like in order to fit in, as well as to keep Indigo going, I had to say and do things I really didn't believe, which was damaging to my soul. Overall, I'd describe the entire experience as soul crushing and dehumanizing.

Interestingly, I would use the very same adjectives to describe my experience as a child in school, which is why I started Indigo in the first place. In school I chose to become something I was not to achieve "success" in a rigid system that rewarded sameness and puppetry. I *was* rewarded for that success, but at great personal expense. After spending years finding myself again and subsequently starting a company to prevent education from being a soul-crushing experience for anyone else, I could not bear to play the funding game required to "win" in the business world. I tried, dear God; I tried so hard because I thought I needed the money. But beyond a trickle that came in when I was in most dire need, all that effort amounted to no monetary avail and began to damage my soul once more in the process. I was desperate to find a way out of the cycle.

Shortly after pastor Rich shared the term spiritual entrepreneurship with me, I decided to stop trying to raise money. I needed to ponder this new reality and see if there was another way to think about capital within the new framework. However, because I was already a finalist in a venture capital (VC) contest for women, I decided to go through with the contest and see what I could learn.

At first, everything seemed like a typical VC experience. The investor panel response was all criticism I'd heard before: lack of focus, a strange cap table, and lack of hockey stick growth.[3,4] Basically, Indigo didn't fit into the standard funding model box. Although none of these critiques were new to me, I found them frustrating because I could not easily change them, nor did they have anything to do with the real mission or work of my company. The advice didn't help me acquire customers, find investors who *were* aligned, or generate revenue.

The three principles of venture capital align to our failing education system

However, with that experience I realized that my real frustration was not with these investors or this contest. Despite being completely unhelpful, the advisors were respectful. The "aha" moment was realizing that they, too, were bound by the prison of the system that venture capital had created. Somehow, most professional investors feel compelled to follow the rules, parameters, and precedent that venture capitalists (VCs) have set. It is my observation that this deeply American system uses three decision-making techniques to the detriment of fairness or even innovative progress:

1. Exclusivity
2. Ranking and Sorting
3. Money

---

[3] A cap table is a list of all the securities your company has issued and who owns them: Jenna Lee, "What is a cap table?" *The Carta Blog*, October 08, 2019, https://carta.com/blog/what-is-a-cap-table/.

[4] Adam Hayes, "Hockey Stick Chart," *Investopedia*, updated October 23, 2021, https://www.investopedia.com/terms/h/hockey-stick-chart.asp.

I couldn't help but chuckle when I first realized this. Everyone thinks of venture capitalists as so innovative, but in fact they have a very canned formula. Entrepreneurs are limited in their innovation and joy of creation by being bound to such a system. Yet in another stroke of irony (or by design), it just so happens that these three drivers are precisely what mainstream education is fixated on as well.

It's very odd to me that both venture capital and education are fixated on a way of being that produces very poor results and limits creativity and experimentation. In both systems, it is only the outliers that drive real progress. For example, nine out of ten start-up companies fail.[5] This is true even among venture-backed companies that are being infused with tens of millions of dollars.

In the education realm, we are failing students and limiting innovation by aligning with similar principles to venture capital. The ideas of exclusivity, ranking and sorting kids, and top-down funding models promote administrative bloat and mediocrity. As Dr. Todd Rose at Harvard noted, "The education system serves no one."[6]

As in business, the divide in education between the rich and poor is only growing wider. Most adults in the system, from the superintendent to the teacher, are completely exhausted, overwhelmed, and underappreciated and were so even before the pandemic affected so much in education, and in life. Among students, mental health issues and suicides are growing at unprecedented rates.[7]

---

[5] For one article discussing start-up failure rates, see Kryil Kotashev, "Startup Failure Rate: How Many Startups Fail and Why?" *Failory's Blog*, updated January 09, 2022, https://www.failory.com/blog/startup-failure-rate.

[6] Todd Rose, "The Myth of Average," Filmed June 20, 2013 in Sonoma County, CA, TEDx Talks video, 18:27, https://www.youtube.com/watch?v=4eBmyttcfU4.

[7] For one of the numerous articles on youth mental health, see "The Student Mental Health Crisis: Resources for Reporters," *Education Writers Association*, October 14, 2022, https://ewa.org/news-explainers/

The cost of higher education is increasing exponentially, while relative earnings have remained flat in this country since the 1970s.[8] Our education system cannot be defined as a success by any of these measures.

Those engaged in a spiritual enterprise must look beyond these failing venture capital values when figuring out how they will operate. Let's unpack the pillars of venture capital—exclusivity, ranking and sorting, and money and contrast them with the principles of spiritual capital—inclusivity, enoughness, and value, examining how a spiritual entrepreneur can move beyond these principles into something better suited for creativity, purpose, and lasting impact.

Exclusivity

Exclusivity is "the practice of excluding or not admitting other things."[9] Most people must be kept out of an organization, school, or club for it to be exclusive. Ivy League colleges are one of the most prominent examples of exclusivity—they proudly publish low acceptance rates and the smaller the acceptance rate, the better. Another example might be a golf course with a very high membership fee, thus making it attainable only to those with the most money.

Exclusivity is a powerful force in society that stands in direct opposition to God's way of inclusivity. Marty Solomon exclaims,

---

[8] Camilo Maldonado, "Price of College Increasing Almost 8 Times Faster than Wages," *Forbes*, July 24, 2018, https://www.forbes.com/sites/camilomaldonado/2018/07/24/price-of-college-increasing-almost-8-times-faster-than-wages/.

[9] *Google's English Dictionary*, provided by *Oxford Languages*, s.v. "define exclusivity," Google search.

"Exclusivity is the anti-gospel!"[10] He argues that the message of inclusivity is present from the very beginning of the Bible and a missing message in most of mainstream Christianity. There are so many illustrations of how God chooses to bring people in rather than shut them out. Some of the most powerful examples can be seen in the life of Jesus on earth. He shocked the wealthy, powerful, and privileged people by seeking out the marginalized of society, the ones who were usually excluded: the poor, the sick, the women, the sinners. He even included "tarnished" women in his own lineage.[11]

Ultimately, Jesus made the way for all to be included in his kingdom when the veil in the temple, the barrier between man and God, was torn when Jesus died.[12] Sadly, people often do not follow Jesus's example of being inclusive. People seek exclusivity for three reasons:

1. Many people fundamentally believe in zero sum games, which mean that when someone wins, the other must lose. Zero sum games assume a fixed number of resources. They cannot envision living in a world where all can thrive.

2. Many like feeling that they are better than others. Living in and visiting places that are nicer and more expensive than others gives them a feeling of security and superiority. It also appears that people equate wealth with intelligence and there is a

---

[10] Marty Solomon and Brent Billings, "Galatians – Two Women, Two Covenants," December 12, 2019, in *BEMA Discipleship Podcast Episode 147*, podcast, MP3 audio, https://www.bemadiscipleship.com/147.

[11] See Matthew 1:1-17. Matthew mentions the following women (women were not typically mentioned in lineages at the time): Tamar, a Canaanite who pretended to be a prostitute to sleep with her father-in-law, who had wronged her; Rahab, a prostitute by profession who saved the Hebrew spies; Ruth, a foreign woman from the tribe of Moab who followed her mother-in-law back to Bethlehem; Uriah's wife, Bathsheba, who slept with David while her husband was at war; and Mary, the mother of Jesus who was pregnant by the Holy Spirit before getting married.

[12] See Matthew 27:50-51.

general feeling that those with financial means are smarter, adding to the superiority complex.

3. Many believe that being in an exclusive crowd will lead to more opportunities, status, fame, and money, which often bears out true in our current paradigm.

Sadly, religion has been one of the greatest culprits of promoting a culture of exclusivity. You are either in the club that is going to heaven or you are going to burn in hell. A woman I know who had been working to provide food and care for homeless individuals was recently sent a statement of faith by a church that supports her work financially. She was required to sign the statement to continue receiving funding. However, she couldn't bring herself to sign because it essentially said that the very people she loved and served were not worthy of heaven because they didn't believe the same theology the church espoused.

This is not an extreme example. And religion is not the only area where we see exclusivity: it is happening all around us, in almost every facet of life, with devastating consequences. As I mentioned before, nothing screams exclusivity more than Ivy League universities. There is a wealthy high school in California that lost six precious seniors to a group suicide when they didn't get into Stanford. A recent college bribery scandal that involved several celebrities highlights the extent to which parents will go to get their kids into the exclusive clubs these schools represent.[13]

---

[13] Elissa Nadworny, "Does It Matter Where You Go To College? Some Context for the Admissions Scandal," *National Public Radio*, March 13, 2019, https://www.npr.org/2019/03/13/702973336/does-it-matter-where-you-go-to-college-some-context-for-the-admissions-scandal.

While I did not go to an Ivy, it was apparent that having degrees from more prestigious universities, along with the color of my skin, gave me credibility and access to networks not typically in the reach of someone from my background. The name of the institution and credential obtained seemed to matter most to others, not who I was as a person or my authentic learning. This experience made such an impression on me that Indigo was initially focused on evolving the mindset of postsecondary institutions. I wondered what would happen if these premier institutions were to switch their perspectives to that of inclusivity. I hypothesized that a radical shift in admissions policies at top universities would produce a trickle-down effect on the public high school system, relieving pressure on high-achieving students and creating more pathways for diverse students to access these networks.

In answering this question, I attended college admissions conferences and spoke with the head of admissions at Princeton, Stanford, MIT, the University of Michigan, and Cal Poly. What I discovered was eye-opening: every one of those admissions leaders wanted more inclusivity, cared deeply about diversity, and tried their best to focus on the individual. Many were dismayed at how homogeneous their applicant pools were, as the standards to attend are simply unattainable by most underprivileged public high school students. However, despite their intentions, none of them had a solution to the exclusivity problem as they saw the system as too entrenched and low acceptance rates as critical to the institution's survival.

I understand the dilemma, as there currently isn't a way in our existing system to maintain prestige and value people's uniqueness at scale. If students I talk to are pursuing Ivy Leagues, I often encourage them to do so, especially if they come from diverse backgrounds. The benefit of the exclusive network typically outweighs the possible adverse effects of being immersed in an exclusive environment. In many ways, this is why there are so many statistical advantages to obtaining a college degree. The social capital argument is important and very real, especially around economic connectedness.[14] I want to make it clear that I am not discouraging people from seizing opportunities as they arise, but rather emphasizing the importance of raising awareness about the situation at hand. Awareness may help people in positions of power better understand their privilege and not judge others without similar social capital. It has certainly supported me in not taking my degrees or the degrees of others too seriously, placing undue importance on external accomplishments.

Exclusivity in venture capital

Venture capital is the dominant source of start-up funding in America. VC firms in the US raised a record-shattering $128.3 billion in 2021.[15] VC investments are highly coveted by start-up CEOs because the amount of financing you receive allows your company to quickly scale and win a significant portion of market share. While there is a cost to doing business with venture capitalists (often, losing control of your company), there is also the possibility of great reward. VCs are incentivized to turn their profits over quickly, and they have a network of buyers that acquire businesses. Although most venture-backed companies still fail, the ones that make it can have returns of ten times the investment amount or more.

But I don't think people realize how exclusive the VC club really is. In his TEDx Talk, "The Kidnapping of the American Dream," Brian

---

[14] Raj Chetty et al., "Social Capital and Economic Mobility," Non-Technical Research Summary, *Opportunity Insights*, August, 2022, https://opportunityinsights.org/wp-content/uploads/2022/07/.

[15] Priyamvada Mathur, "Six charts that show 2021's record year for US venture capital," *Pitchbook*, January 19, 2022, https://pitchbook.com/news/articles/2021-record-year-us-venture-capital-six-charts#. See also: Cassie Ann Hodges, "US Venture Capital Investment Surpasses $130 Billion in 2019 for Second Consecutive Year," *National Ventura Capital Association (NVCA)*, January 14, 2022, https://nvca.org/pressreleases/us-venture-capital-investment-surpasses-130-billion-in-2019-for-second-consecutive-year/.

MacMahon shares the statistics in grim detail.[16] He explains how the VC world is still largely an Ivy League "good old boy" club. Obtaining funding depends more on your connections and having a wealthy background than on the "hard work of creative individuals." He states there is a 0% chance of founding a billion-dollar tech company if you grew up in a low-income area. There is also a much lower chance if you are a Black, Latino or a woman. Black and Latino founders receive about 2.5% of VC funding and women still receive less than 10% of venture capital (and most of these women are from that exclusive club).[17]

Despite initiatives to change these statistics, it is not happening at the scale needed to make a difference in the existing system. And even if it did, do we really want to support the VC model of grow, grow, grow at any cost? Venture firms pump huge amounts of money into companies, so any founding money becomes meaningless and founders lose control. Then VCs do whatever it takes to raise the company's valuation so they can exit quickly. Company sales are typically made to one of their friends or colleagues—that way everyone in the club generates a sizable return, which feeds the cycle of exclusivity.

My intention is not to vilify VCs. They are operating in the way that is natural based on current systems. Many of those involved in venture capital are good people who want to make a difference in the world and care about what they are doing. However, the fundamental system of operating is far removed from the intrinsic values and goals of a spiritual entrepreneur, and the exclusive model limits diversity.

---

[16] Brian MacMahon, "The Kidnapping of the American Dream," July 19, 2016, in University of California Irvine, TEDx Talks, video, https://www.youtube.com/watch?v=Y6f7lFy0oW0.

[17] Galen Gruman, "Minority tech startups in the US have seen almost no progress in VC funding," *ComputerWorld*, October 07, 2020, https://www.computerworld.com/article/3584734/minority-tech-startups-in-the-us-have-seen-almost-no-progress-in-vc-funding.html.

Increasing equity and reducing bias through inclusivity

Somehow the idea of numerical valuation has been tied to the equity conversation. We have adopted a one-sided belief that if you reduce a person, company, job candidate, or student down to numbers, you can somehow be more fair, equitable, or impartial. However, evidence points to the opposite being the case.

I once met with a women's angel investing group that had adopted venture capital metrics to exclude certain founders because they felt like this method was less biased and more fair. Imagine if these women were instead investing in a way that was decidedly more feminine—using their intuition, empathy, and love. What if the group introduced investors to female founders who aligned with their heart-based interests? The investors could develop relationships with the founders, become engaged in the companies, and get to know their work intimately.

Doesn't this sound more exciting and fulfilling than an "impartial" number? Perhaps this approach could also increase equity and provide more chances for founders who don't fit the dominant success paradigms, as often spiritual entrepreneurs do not. It would certainly include people who typically would be excluded based on their non-conformation to profit goals.

The irony in the case I referred to was that the women involved were using dollars traditionally used in philanthropy for the investment. Any return of principal at all would have been a greater monetary return than philanthropy. Therefore, taking a chance on any one of these female founders was really no chance at all. The investors had nothing to lose and everything to gain.

A more feminine approach would not eliminate the need for an organizational structure to support these investors. The group could be more involved in crucial ways such as teaching a wider range of potential investment targets about different deal structures, helping with required paperwork, and developing camaraderie as the members share the joy in their investing pursuits. The group does some of this, but it could be more powerful if aligned to the spiritual principal of inclusivity. The group acts collectively, but within that, each woman could contribute in a way that is best aligned with her own sense of purpose. Wouldn't it be interesting to experiment and see what would happen if people were to invest this way instead?

Ranking and Sorting

Exclusivity goes hand in hand with ranking and sorting. The whole process of ranking and sorting companies and founders may seem like a necessary process in the investment world. However, just like deeming a kid's intelligence by their SAT score, ranking and sorting is a one-dimensional measure at best.[18] In God's kingdom value is inherent. It is an irrevocable truth of all of God's creation. Thus, ranking and sorting is not necessary because everyone belongs, there is enough for all, and each person is enough by simply being who they truly are.

As a CEO trying to raise capital, win contests, and cut deals, I am constantly being ranked and sorted. For example, when I asked for feedback as to why Indigo wasn't selected for an investment program,

---

[18] Ranking and Sorting is also known as "tracking" in education. KnowledgeWorks published a provoking article sharing the history and negative impact of this inequitable practice: Eric Toshalis, EdD and Virgel Hammonds, "Let's Face It: Tracking Is Intentional Systemic Inequity," *KnowledgeWorks*, November 02, 2021, https://knowledgeworks.org/resources/tracking-is-intentional-systemic-inequity/.

they said they didn't have any specifics because they used a scoring process. Again, in an effort to be "fair," they scored and ranked the twenty finalists. The eight with the most "points" got the investment. This was painful because I felt reduced to a number. I didn't even know what my "number" was, just that it wasn't enough. It was also entirely unhelpful, as I didn't learn anything useful for how I could improve in the future.

The whole purpose of Indigo is to move the education system away from viewing kids through the lens of numbers (test scores). How many children feel like they are not enough because they cannot score a high enough number on the SAT? Likewise, I wonder how many spiritual entrepreneurs feel inadequate because they are being measured by factors incongruent with their core mission and values.

It's disappointing that we continue to rank and sort kids, adults, companies, institutions, and ideas numerically when people seem to agree that the most important things in life cannot be quantified. Can we measure love? Or connection? Or beauty? Or the feeling of being alive? As Anthony J. DeAngelo, co-chair of the Commission on Public Relations Education, once said, "The most important things in life aren't things."[19]

I believe one of the reasons Indigo has experienced challenges raising capital is so that I could viscerally feel what it's like being ranked and sorted by measures that don't mean anything to me. It is the same pain felt when I go into schools and look into the eyes of teachers and students who are also ranked and sorted by numbers that have nothing to do with who they are or the things that matter to them. Empathy increases from failures and I'm grateful for opportunities to grow.

---

[19] See https://www.brainyquote.com/quotes/anthony_j_dangelo_377827.

Enoughness replacing ranking and sorting

In many cases the metrics by which people are ranked and sorted directly tie to being able to gain entrance to exclusive systems or organizations. It's based on the flawed belief that there is not enough for everyone so we must rank people by "merit" and those at the bottom receive nothing. Even more sinister is an internalized belief that people at the bottom *deserve* nothing.

Some of you will recognize this line of thinking as scarcity mindset. According to *Business Insider*, scarcity mindset is "a belief that wealth is limited, and that one can run out or never have enough."[20] WebMD cites several studies tying this way of thinking to medical conditions such as a lowering of your IQ, limiting your brain function, and making impulse control harder.[21]

Most articles contrast scarcity with abundance. *Forbes* defines abundance mindset as "the paradigm that there is plenty out there for everybody."[22] I completely agree with abundance. There are many fantastic Bible verses on abundance. Here is one of my favorites:

> And God is able to bless you abundantly, so that in all things at all times, having all that you need, you will abound in every good work. (2 Corinthians 9:8)

---

[20] Aly J. Yale, "What to know about the scarcity mindset and how it affects women and their finances — and 6 ways to avoid it," *Business Insider*, May 07, 2022, https://www.businessinsider.com/personal-finance/scarcity-mindset.

[21] WebMD Editorial Contributors, "What Is Scarcity Mentality," reviewed by Dan Brennan, MD, *WebMD*, updated October 25, 2021, https://www.webmd.com/mental-health/what-is-scarcity-mentality.

[22] Caroline Castrillon, "5 Ways to Go from a Scarcity to Abundance Mindset," *Forbes*, July 12, 2020, https://www.forbes.com/sites/carolinecastrillon/2020/07/12/5-ways-to-go-from-a-scarcity-to-abundance-mindset/?sh=446ffa671197.

Unfortunately, God's promises of abundance are often used in unhealthy ways that promote inequity and justify the system of "haves and have-nots" rather than supporting inclusivity and the sharing of wealth. I feel like the word is so overused, that I chose the word *enoughness* rather than abundance to convey the meaning. Enoughness isn't necessarily about getting rich; it's about the idea that God provides for our needs, and it is our responsibility to share with those who don't have enough any abundance God has blessed us with.

If VC funding and philanthropic giving were more equally distributed, there would likely be enough money for all promising women and minority-led ventures. Investors' risk would be diversified as well. Financing systems (including many large philanthropic gifts) are so obsessed with scale that smaller, hyper-localized companies are overlooked. In many cases these smaller companies provide better customer service, drive more innovation, and support local economies more than huge unicorn-style money-making machines. It is unfortunate that the need for exclusivity is so high that many promising businesses don't have enough because they are essentially sorted out.

Money

The song "Money Makes the World Go Round" feels very true in our current society. In the world of venture capital, return on investment (ROI) is king. VCs have a great deal of pressure to pour enormous amounts of capital into select exclusive companies and drive them to the fastest exit possible in order to do it all over again. Traditional venture capital is explicit about the need for a return; there is really no other goal. Spiritual entrepreneurs focus, instead, on spiritual capital as measured by love expanding and others receiving value from their goods or services, rather than focusing on personal monetary rewards.

The idea of scaling a company to gain significant market share goes hand in hand with making money. The more a company can dominate a market, the more money it can make, and the more control it has over consumer behavior and market trends. This ensures continued ability to scale.

Only recently have companies been able to achieve "world domination" through technology. Information technology giants such as Alphabet (Google), Amazon, Apple, Meta (Facebook), and Microsoft are the primary examples of companies that have achieved this status (known collectively as "Big Tech"). In 2019 Big Tech generated $900 billion in revenue. If we compared Big Tech's earnings to the nations of the world, it would rank eighteenth on the list of largest countries by GDP, well above Saudi Arabia and just below the Netherlands.[23] The goal of many aspiring tech founders is to become the next global tech company, and the goal of most VCs is to find and scale that next big tech company.

Numbers like this are difficult to comprehend and have really raised the bar of success in entrepreneurship. Big Tech has also created a whole new crop of celebrities, and a class of workers making $200k per year with an opulent standard of corporate perks that only a company of that size can offer. In essence, Big Tech has created a new reality that many entrepreneurs strive for and measure themselves against.

This is not all bad. I'm grateful that I can search on Google, use Microsoft's Office suite, order Italian flour on Amazon, and connect with my friends on Facebook or FaceTime. Moreover, these

---

[23] Daniyal Malik, "How Big Tech Companies Are Earning Billions to Beat the Economy of Whole Countries," *Digital Information World*, August 25, 2020, https://www.digitalinformationworld.com/2020/08/how-big-tech-companies-are-earning-billions-to-beat-the-economy-of-big-countries.html.

companies do have extensive corporate social responsibility programs, donate to nonprofits, and have provided opportunities for smaller businesses to sell their services and products. There is always a delicate balance when considering the pros and cons of progress. However, I do think Big Tech has only perpetuated the view that money is the main goal of business and that founders who make billions are more valuable and more worthy of our respect and adoration than others. The average person believes it, too. Think about how you view and treat a wealthy person versus a homeless person begging on the street.

Most venture capitalists I've encountered also seem to believe that about themselves. In subtle or not-so-subtle ways, they make it clear that they believe they are smarter, more important, and more worthy than the start-up founders they invest in. But the truth is that if the start-up founders weren't willing to work incredibly hard and put up with the venture capitalists, the VCs wouldn't have the returns that make their system exist. The founders are the real reason the VCs have wealth, just like the employees are the reason why start-up companies succeed, and just like customers are the reason businesses grow at all. All the pieces are interconnected: this is part of the holistic nature of value that spiritual entrepreneurs recognize and embrace. Sadly, interconnectedness is not fully realized in today's model of money-driven ventures.

Self-interest and wetiko

The "more is better" and "bigger is better" philosophy perpetuated by venture capital and big tech has a much more insidious effect than simply making people arrogant. It feeds "a psychological force within the unconscious mind that predisposes us toward unwholesome impulses such as the thirst for power, control, greed, and jealousy."[24] This force was first recognized by Native Americans, who saw it as a mind virus or cannibalistic spirit. Many indigenous cultures have words for it; I like to use the Algonquin word *wetiko*. The virus is caused by the illusion of separation from others and all things. Indigenous populations thought white settlers were infected with wetiko, based on self-interested and greedy actions, lacking a sense of interconnectedness.

Wetiko feels like an insatiable hunger. This hunger "lulls humanity into a trancelike dance of mindless consumption."[25] It is the opposite of the spiritual principle of enoughness. With wetiko, there is never enough. In fact, wetiko amplifies negative emotions, turning anger into rage and fear into panic. Now that I've been exposed to the term, I see it everywhere—in myself, business, news, consumerism, etc. Whenever I feel myself focusing on my fears, scarcity, and victimhood, I know wetiko is at play. It's a feeling of unraveling.

The counterintuitive thing about wetiko is that you can't fight it externally, in society. Fighting it only feeds it. It thrives off people hating and judging each other. I can feel a palpable shift inside myself when I start condemning people in venture capital versus observing the reality and then sending love to the system. My condemnation only makes wetiko stronger and makes me weaker. The constant battle between feeding the system and forgiving the system is ongoing.

Money and business can quickly lead the entrepreneur to wetiko, without self-awareness. A few paragraphs barely scratch the surface,

---

[24] Paul Levy, *Wetiko: Healing the Mind-Virus That Plagues Our World*, Forward by Larry Dossey, M.D. (Inner Traditions, 2021).

[25] Sherri Mitchell, *Sacred Instructions: Indigenous Wisdom for Living Spirit-Based Change* (North Atlantic Books, 2018), 47-48.

but wetiko is an essential element to the whole spiritual entrepreneurship conversation. The concept sheds light on the profound nature of the problem of greed and how it has permeated society subconsciously.

Social impact investing in its current form is not the answer

There has been a groundswell of support for a new type of investing called social impact investing. Social impact investing refers to "investments made with the intention to generate positive, measurable social and environmental impact alongside a financial return."[26] There are many conferences and groups that focus on this today, with the most notable being SOCAP Global.[27] SOCAP is short for socially responsible capital. The idea of using capital to make the world a better place and deliver non-monetary value is incredibly powerful and appeals to people all over the world.

I have deep respect and great love for social entrepreneurs who can run sustainable, profitable businesses while authentically doing good. They are doing God's work and it's not easy for them. Sadly, the capital side to the social impact industry has, in many aspects, become even more misguided than traditional venture capital. When the idea of doing good is placed in an extrinsic framework where money is still king, the original intent of socially responsible investment becomes distorted, allowing investors to feel even more justified in the pursuit of ROI while patting themselves on the back for being "good."

---

[26] "What You Need to Know about Impact Investing," *Global Impact Investing Network*, https://thegiin.org/impact-investing/need-to-know/.
[27] "About Us - SOCAP Global," *SOCAP GOBAL*: https://socapglobal.com/about-us/.

As a social entrepreneur, instead of having to just meet the money return criteria, you also must do something good in the world. Therefore, your company valuation will typically be lower. As social businesses don't tend to make as much money generally, they are automatically worth less from a financial standpoint and, therefore, tend to be evaluated more harshly. I had one billionaire impact investor say, "I get my returns and you melt my heart in the process." That conversation still disturbs me.

I had another conversation with a very wealthy investor who proclaimed to be a devout Christian. He claimed to have been blessed by God so he could give to charity. He decided not to invest in Indigo because he said that God told him that he should only invest in companies in which he could make $100 million or more so he could get his large returns and then give more away. That logic doesn't make sense to me. I left feeling disheartened at how the message of Christianity is too often twisted in the eyes of those with wealth and power to suit their own interests.

We can't help but focus on the wealthy

A problem with monetary focus is that people who start funds or social impact events must focus on the investors—the people who have the wealth—instead of on the entrepreneurs they want to help. They need the people who have the wealth to attend their events and invest in their funds, or they will cease to exist. The net impact of this is a continued, misplaced focus on the wealthy as the source of value instead of on the start-up companies, innovation, or entrepreneurs.

I have seen this pattern at every social impact event I've attended over the past ten years. For example, there is a popular education conference that caters to the wealthy, powerful, and famous. Thousands of people come and pay thousands of dollars each to have access to education technology (EdTech) investors and funders. There is very little focus on or access to the conference for the everyday people doing the day-to-day hard work in schools.

The conference is sold out every year and is considered the most exclusive event in education. Former presidents, Bill Gates, Richard Branson, and countless other big names have keynoted there. I've attended for years because it seemed that everyone I needed to network with was there. However, the energy I encounter there always leaves me feeling empty in my soul and physically, mentally, and emotionally exhausted.

I now understand that the reason I'm so impacted by energy, in particular the energy around money, is because I'm a highly sensitive person, or an empath: a person who is highly sensitive to the feelings of others.[28] However, even non-empaths struggle with the atmosphere of this conference and the difficulty of truly doing good in the education space in general. Countless conversations with other EdTech founders confirm that making a lasting impact involves far more roadblocks than perpetuating the existing one-size-fits-all system.

Money follows existing power structures

In education there is a clear divide between companies that are making money off the existing system (like textbook, testing, and school furniture supply companies) and start-ups that are trying to make a profit while also attempting to shift the existing system to something more empowering for students and educators. Because the education system is focused on getting people through the system *en masse*,

---

[28] I discuss empaths in detail in chapter 6.

companies and products that help schools do this more efficiently get purchased at high prices but have little real impact. I call these "check the boxes more efficiently" products. They deliver little value to students. Companies trying to do something differently and offer real value helping people can barely give their product away for free.

One of my board members said it best:

> Sheri, you are trying to get someone to take a bus when they already have planes. What you really need to offer them is a private jet. Everyone would choose a private jet over a commercial airline, but no one would choose Greyhound.

He's right in one sense but missing the point slightly: in reality, none of the known modes of transport will get them there. People are resistant to change, and true transformation is only wrought through struggle. It's a rare person in power who will choose the difficult path to an unknown, but potentially better, place over taking the private jet to a known destination that makes sense to them.

As in education, investment systems have momentum that cascades down from the largest events to the smaller, much less glamorous events. There is a Colorado event for social impact that follows this pattern. To have a little exhibit booth at the event, companies must go through a long ranking and sorting process (again, so the organization can appear exclusive), spend hundreds of dollars on materials for a booth, and still pay the same admission fee that investors pay to get into the conference.

During the event, there is no way to meet investors other than by chance. Nor is there a way for investors to easily find the booths of companies working in impact areas they care about. So many entrepreneurs leave dejected because the event focuses on entertaining investors but does little or nothing to help the entrepreneurs. This is despite the marketing and stated focus of the event, which was to help grow social impact organizations in the state.

I sound like I am complaining, and that is sometimes true. I am guilty of judgment and bitterness sometimes from being exposed to such events year after year. I certainly haven't worked through all my own personal issues yet, but I feel like it's important to bring these patterns up so other spiritual entrepreneurs don't feel alone, crazy, or wrong.

In most cases, these organizations and events are run by people who are good-hearted, care about women and/or social entrepreneurs, and want to improve society. However, they fail to see how the adulation of money does not align with the spiritual principles of inclusivity, enoughness, and value but instead perpetuates the same biased system they are trying to improve. They are trapped within the same system of exclusivity, ranking and sorting, and money. They too must "bow" to it to be successful.

Funding alternatives to institutional capital

It was difficult for me as an entrepreneur to realize there really aren't many capital alternatives for people starting businesses, especially those without connections or a pedigree. The Small Business Administration (SBA), which is supposed to be the answer for Main Street America, requires that you personally guarantee your own assets as well as have good credit to receive a small amount of capital.

Under the SBA scenario, if your little gift shop in a struggling town goes out of business because Walmart moves in and you can't pay your loan, you lose your house. However, a VC can invest $100 million into a greed-based business model with a narcissistic founder and when it all comes down, they walk away, and everyone is still rich.

WeWork is a great example of this, even more so after the recent announcement that WeWork founder Adam Neumann raised $350 million from venture capital for a new real estate company.[29]

Angel investing is a viable alternative to institutional funding, but "angels" are increasingly being trained to use VC-like criteria that doesn't make sense for many businesses. Moreover, amounts are small, and in many markets, it takes a substantial amount of money to scale because of the nature of the system. If you don't fit into the VC bucket, it's unlikely that you will ever have enough capital to compete on a national scale.

I'd love to imagine completely new funding models for spiritual entrepreneurs. For example, my husband envisions Banking 2.0, in which our central bank would sponsor Community Enterprise Funds. Such funds would be managed by local citizens who invest money to help launch enterprises that are not profit oriented but serve the needs of the community.[30] This could fund spiritual entrepreneurs at scale.

One of my favorite stories in the Bible (Matthew 2:1-12) is the Magi coming to find baby Jesus and offer him gifts of great symbolic and monetary value. These wise men were led by a star that foretold a great king. When they arrived and found a small family in humble conditions (not at Jesus's birth as is often portrayed in Nativity scenes), they could have turned away. There was nothing external to make them think a great king had been born. However, they followed their hearts, believed in the signs, and gave their gifts. Their gifts were really a great investment in the future, one that likely allowed Jesus's

---

[29] Fernando Alfonso III, "$350 million for WeWork co-founder shows how broken and biased venture capital is," *National Public Radio*, August 26, 2022,
https://www.npr.org/2022/08/26/1119415180/wework-flow-adam-neumann-vc-venture-capital-350-million-gender-bias-horowitz.

[30] See https://www.thefoundationforabettereconomy.org/.

family to escape and live in Egypt. This type of investment, where investors follow their hearts because of a belief in something greater than themselves, would revolutionize current standards for investment and open the door for human-centered innovation on our planet.

MacKenzie Scott (Jeff Bezos's ex-wife) is a great example of a new type of funder. In her recent giving campaign, she threw out all the rules of organized philanthropy and simply gave money without any strings attached to nonprofits she felt were meeting a real need. She did not have formal ties with most of these organizations but saw strong leadership, a need, and low access to capital. In this highly efficient and altruistic manner, she distributed $4.1 billion in four months.[31] She was led to give by factors that didn't necessarily make sense by standard funding model rules: she gave where she felt it was important to give. I'd love to see a whole new generation of MacKenzie Scotts giving to smaller nonprofits, investing in spiritual entrepreneurs, and starting companies and organizations themselves.

You may be thinking, "Sheri, your examples don't make sense; the Magi and MacKenzie are philanthropists, not investors!" You are correct in the strict definition of the terms, but in the realm of spiritual entrepreneurship, current definitions no longer suffice. From God's perspective, the definitions *never* made sense. Classes of funders were created mainly for tax purposes; they have little bearing on the heart of the person, which is what God cares about. Some money-focused investors have the hearts of philanthropists, with few strings attached to their funding. Plenty of philanthropists possess hearts that are about themselves: they seek to make a name for their foundations or manipulate those they invest in to focus on *their* agenda.

---

[31] There are many amazing articles about MacKenzie Scott. This one is from her own site: MacKenzie Scott, "Seeding by Ceding," *Medium*, June 15, 2021, https://mackenzie-scott.medium.com/seeding-by-ceding-ea6de642bf.

Spiritual capital redefines value

Spiritually minded investors care about the receiver and who benefits from the receiver's efforts. For example, you might be funding an entrepreneurial venture (either a for-profit or a non-profit) that provides tangible rewards for the venture's customers—things like food, clean water or better education, but for you as the giver, the reward is intangible. In this instance, a spiritual funder prioritizes the impact of their gift on others, rather than what they personally receive from it. The emphasis shifts to supporting the growth of humanity, which becomes the true measure of the return on investment.

In this case, money is replaced by true value. Since God values each of us infinitely, spiritual capital values a return on the physical, emotional and spiritual well-being of humanity and our planet.

What if we stopped comparing children and assigning numerical values to humans? What if we even stopped defining our companies by their numerical valuation? One of the questions I get asked most is, "What is the current valuation of your company?" I understand why you need a monetary valuation for buying and selling. However, just like an SAT score tells you almost nothing about a child, a monetary valuation does not even begin to describe the value of a company from a spiritual perspective.

Dr. Sue Gleeson provides another perspective on valuation:

> I don't think that the amount of money made doing a particular venture is correlated to the rightness or value of the venture. The rightness of doing something seems to me to be something we assess inside ourselves. What's the feeling of fulfillment and meaning I am

getting from doing what I am doing? If it's a lot... then the venture has value![32]

Conclusion: Refocusing Humanity's ROI

It's extremely difficult to live out the three dimensions of spiritual entrepreneurship while trying to succeed in an exclusive framework that ranks and sorts you. The emphasis on money as the primary objective, even if it's a shared goal in the realm of social impact investing, creates a sense of conflict for individuals who prioritize their spiritual journey.

Money for the sake of money has no purpose. Paul said, "For the love of money is a root of all kinds of evil" (1Timothy 6:10). Money itself is not bad, and all entrepreneurs need it. However, loving money leads to no good, but our current system rewards the love of money and those who accumulate it.

Money only has use if it is put to work to evolve humanity and to grow the general prosperity. Thomas Keating, an American Catholic monk known as one of the principal developers of Centering Prayer, describes God's priority when it comes to innovation and money:

> God's top priority is the creation of a world in which the goods of the earth are equitably distributed, where no one is forgotten or left out, and where no one can rest until everyone has enough to eat, the oppressed have been liberated, and justice and peace are the norm among the nations and religions of the world. Until then, even the joy of transforming union is incomplete.

---

[32] Susan Gleeson. Email to author, 2021.

> The commitment to the spiritual journey is not a commitment to pure joy, but to taking responsibility for the whole human family, its needs and destiny. We are not our own; we belong to everyone else.[33]

Spiritual entrepreneurs are actively working toward the vision of liberation, justice, and peace for humanity that Keating describes. They do this by focusing on the principles of spiritual capital rather than chasing venture capital. The following table characterizes the difference between venture and spiritual capital.

Venture Capital	Spiritual Capital
Exclusivity	Inclusivity
Ranking & Sorting	Enoughness[34]
Money	Value

God's way of inclusivity is directly opposed to the exclusivity favored in venture capital. The ranking and sorting methods for determining who receives funding is unnecessary when we look at how much abundance comes from God. With God, there is enough. He created each person uniquely; how can one rank or sort and compare what is not meant to be compared? Being your unique self is enough. In the eyes of God each person is intrinsically valuable; it has nothing to do with how much money they have. Money is an artificial construct we value in a manner that is out of balance with God's values. What God values is clearly love since God is love (1John 4:8).

---

[33] Thomas Keating, *The Mystery of Christ: The Liturgy as Spiritual Experience* (Continuum: 1994), 104.

[34] I know enoughness isn't an official word, but as mentioned earlier in the chapter, I feel like we need a new term for abundance. Abundance is too often correlated with being rich and personally successful, which takes us away from the inherent ideas of abundance I believe God values. Spiritual abundance is more aligned with the concept of enough for all. It's community abundance measured by the inclusion and support of society's most marginalized versus an individualistic concept of accumulation and winning.

Loving the Lord your God with all your heart, soul, strength, and mind, and loving your neighbor as yourself is often cited as the greatest commandment.[35] In Jewish teaching, the middle verse of the Torah (the first five books of the Bible, traditionally attributed to Moses) is regarded as having special significance. This central verse of the Torah concludes with "you shall love your neighbor as yourself. I am the Lord!" (Leviticus 19:18).

Moreover, the *Shema* prayer recited twice daily by Jews around the world includes the commandment to love. The Shema prayer opens with: "Hear O' Israel, the Lord is our God, the Lord is one." In Hebrew "one" is translated as *echad* - the Lord is echad. "To recognize God as echad is to believe that everything and everyone is connected, that we all belong to each other and in the deepest spiritual sense that we are, all of us, cosmically connected."[36] Thus, love is the great spiritual currency connecting us all, not money.

Spiritual entrepreneurs viscerally understand that if we take care of others, we are taking care of ourselves. There are no owners, shareholders, executives, managers, staff, clients, customers, and consumers. Those are all just roles being played. All there is *really* is *us*, and that *us* is part of a larger and more important reality—the reality of love and unity. I'm not fully able to hold the reality of echad yet, so I use the theoretical framework described in the next chapter to expand love from a practical standpoint. This framework of axiology—the study of value—greatly helped me to understand how developing a new paradigm for spiritual entrepreneurship is possible. It naturally promotes inclusivity and enoughness while redefining value toward spiritual capital.

---

[35] See Deuteronomy 6:5, Matthew 22:37, Mark 12:28-31, and Luke 10:27

[36] Harold M. Schulweis, "Echad, Rosh Hashana, 1997," *Valley Beth Shalom*: https://www.vbs.org/worship/meet-our-clergy/rabbi-harold-schulweis/sermons/echad.

CHAPTER 4
VALUING THE INTRINSIC

This chapter outlines formal axiology, the science of value, as a framework for running a spiritual enterprise.[1] This model helps a spiritual entrepreneur reconcile their internal, external, and systemic values into a cohesive whole. The core difference between a spiritual entrepreneur and a conventional entrepreneur is in their definition of "value." The spiritual realm values the intrinsic. Capitalism values the extrinsic. Our government and public institutions, such as the education system, value the systemic.

I first heard about axiology when I was twenty-one, right before I married my first husband. I worked for a national sales director who enlisted me to help him find some assessments for hiring and developing salespeople. In my research, I came across Target Training International (TTI), the company I now partner with for some of Indigo's assessments. One of TTI's brilliant distributors explained to me how all the different assessment instruments and perspectives worked together. I was in awe that a company had developed this level of accuracy and complexity with psychometric tools. People fascinate

---

[1] When I refer to "axiology" throughout this chapter, I am referring to Hartman's Formal Axiology, which is a more refined version of the general branch of philosophy about values that is also referred to as "axiology."

me, and this new understanding formed a lifelong interest in assessments and psychology.

I was particularly fascinated by one assessment, the Hartman Value Profile, because it revealed aspects of myself that were core to both my trauma and my gifts. On the gift side, it showed my keen awareness of people and empathic abilities. It also highlighted my ability to integrate many dimensions of information to solve problems.

On the trauma side, this assessment clearly showed the effects of focusing on grades as my source of value and the constant assault on my own identity from the church. My "sense of self" score was 4.2 on a 10-point scale. I suffered from low self-esteem despite scoring high in self-confidence. My eyes were opened to see how not knowing who *I am* impacted my ability to feel close to God and others. It was also one of the key reasons I married a man I didn't want to: peer pressure led me to value others' opinions more than my own inner knowing.

Overall, I felt in my heart that I was coming to this knowledge because God had a bigger plan. I could never have guessed how all the pieces of my life experiences so perfectly fit together to prepare me for Indigo. In writing this book, it became clear that Hartman's work had formed the basis for Indigo's core philosophy and is now a model for spiritual entrepreneurship.

An Axiological Model for Spiritual Entrepreneurship

Dr. Robert S. Hartman was born in Berlin in 1910. He was forced to leave Nazi Germany in 1932 after speaking out against fascism and writing anti-Nazi articles. Hartman's father was of Jewish heritage, but he was raised Christian, which significantly shaped his worldview.

Dr. Hartman couldn't understand why so many of the "good" people he knew growing up chose to align with evil during the rise of Nazism. This fundamental question compelled him to research the concepts of value and goodness, which became the basis of his life's work.

Hartman had a fascinating life story and worked tirelessly until his death in 1973. He was even nominated for a Nobel Peace Prize. His primary area of study was the science of axiology. Axiology is from the Greek word *axios*, "worthy," and *logos*, "science." It is also called the theory of value.[2] Axiology is intimately connected with various other intellectual fields that also depend on values, such as ethics, aesthetics, and the philosophy of religion. While the term was first used in the early 1900s, the idea of value has been explored extensively since the time of the ancient Greeks.

Most axiological writings are too esoteric for me to wrap my mind around. However, I have used the Hartman Value Profile (HVP) for over twenty years. It is a fifteen-minute mathematically-based assessment tool derived from the hierarchy of values. Dr. Hartman developed the HVP to provide valuable insight into how people view the world and themselves from various dimensions. The results help shed light on decision-making, blind spots, and gifts. Coaching people using the framework of axiology gave me insight into how this theory applies in a practical way to the lives of individuals and organizations. The three dimensions are:

1. Intrinsic
2. Extrinsic
3. Systemic

---

[2] *Encyclopaedia Britannica*, s.v. "Axiology," last modified June 10, 2015, https://www.britannica.com/topic/axiology.

The intrinsic is the dimension of people and self. It is also described as the dimension of "being." It's the spiritual entrepreneur's "heart." When something is being valued from the intrinsic perspective, it has value simply because it exists. It is the recognition that one has value in and of themselves. When Moses asks God what he should say to the Israelites when they ask the name of who sent him, "God said to Moses, 'I am who I am. This is what you are to say to the Israelites: I am has sent me to you'" (Exodus 3:14). God's declaration of himself as YHWH is the most potent example of the intrinsic in the Bible.

The extrinsic is the dimension of tasks and roles. It can also be described as the dimension of "doing." It's the spiritual entrepreneur's "hands." When something is valued from the extrinsic perspective, it has value if it serves a particular function to achieve an external goal. The *kohenim*, or the Jewish priests, are a great example of an extrinsic role in the Bible. Their job was to perform spiritual tasks such as daily sacrifices on behalf of the people. Extrinsic tasks, when done in service of the intrinsic, are holy, and critically important to society.

The systemic is the dimension of systems and direction. It can also be described as the dimension of "thinking." It's the spiritual entrepreneur's "mind." When valuing something from the systemic perspective, it has value if it creates a framework or system to align with. The Jewish Law is an example of the systemic in the Bible. It provided robust guidelines for the nation to organize around. In our lives, we encounter many systems, such as education or healthcare. Systems are necessary for a functioning society and are most helpful when created and maintained to support intrinsic goals. Currently, frameworks such as human-centered systems and human-centered design are being utilized to shift society's focus towards developing products and systems that prioritize the individual's needs.

The following table summarizes Hartman's framework:

Dimension	Focus	Action	Physical
Intrinsic	External: People Internal: Self	Being	Heart
Extrinsic	External: Tasks Internal: Role	Doing	Hands
Systemic	External: Systems Internal: Direction	Thinking	Mind

The table headings refer to the following:

- **Dimension:** each of Hartman's dimensions
- **Focus:** the focus of the dimension both externally (on people, tasks, and systems) and internally (on self, roles, and direction)
- **Action:** how that dimension manifests in people
- **Physical:** a physical representation of each dimension for the spiritual entrepreneur

The Hartman Value Profile gives us insight into how we process the world—specifically, how our brain prioritizes people, tasks, and systems externally—and ourselves, our roles, and our futures internally. We make decisions based on how we perceive the dimensions of both our external and inner worlds. In essence, our perspective on these dimensions shapes our decision-making process.

The basic framework of formal axiology is a simple yet powerful model for spiritual entrepreneurship. Hartman saw the balance between the dimensions and the importance of each one of them. However, he also believed a specific hierarchy of the dimensions would produce ideal results for humanity and our planet. He argued that God created the universe where the intrinsic value is more important than the extrinsic and the systemic. Indeed, it is only because of the intrinsic that we'd ever create the extrinsic or the systemic. An intrinsic-first model keeps the universe in balance and allows for diverse, sustainable life. In his model, the systemic is in service to the extrinsic, and the extrinsic outcomes serve the intrinsic. A simple formula for this reads as follows:

Intrinsic > Extrinsic > Systemic

The formula above is excellent to keep in mind when making decisions and valuing certain aspects of your business. This framework is the basis of many decisions I make. Below are some examples of how this model might work in various realms:

- **Investment:** The entrepreneur (intrinsic) is more important than making money (extrinsic), which is more important than perpetuating a system of exclusivity (systemic). In other words, systemic inclusivity must serve and support the extrinsic funding model, which must in turn serve and support the entrepreneur and those who benefit.

- **Business**: Employees and customers (intrinsic) are more important than making new products or generating profit (extrinsic), which are more important than setting up sales structures and other systems (systemic). In other words, the business systems must serve and support the business goals, which in turn must serve and support the employees and customers.

- **Education:** Students (intrinsic) are more important than getting good test scores (extrinsic), which is more important than preserving the factory model of schooling (systemic). In other words, the education model must serve and support the learning, which must in turn serve and support the students. *Note, this idea is the basis of Indigo.*

Overvaluing the systemic

Let's examine some instances where the intrinsic value is not given the appropriate importance. Hartman's question, "Why did good people in Germany do so many horrific things?" is answered by axiology, which suggests that the emphasis on the systemic at that time was misplaced. Nazi Germany serves as a stark example of what happens when the systemic is used to serve an extrinsic institution that is completely at odds with valuing human life, resulting in atrocities.

Nazism began with Nationalism and concluded in the systemic murder of six million Jews (two-thirds of Europe's Jewish population) through the highly efficient Final Solution. The principal architect of the Final Solution, Heinrich Himmler, appeared to be a genius at implementing systems and, in a sense, "worshiped" systems. He designed an elaborate systemic plan in which millions of people were murdered in a relatively short time.[3]

The entire Nazi regime was based on systemic abuses—systemic fear, systemic brainwashing through organizations like the Hitler Youth, and even systemic racial domination through the *Lebensborn* program for the "birthing" of Aryan-pure babies. When I started researching all the practices by which Hitler attempted to control the populace, I shuddered to realize how close he came to achieving world domination.

---

[3] I highly recommend the Holocaust Encyclopedia from the United States Holocaust Memorial Museum for detailed information: *Holocaust Encyclopedia*, https://encyclopedia.ushmm.org/en.

Overvalued systems allow societies to objectify humans, characterizing them as existing to serve an extrinsic purpose only. In our own country, slavery, institutional racism, and classism are all examples of the systemic being used for destructive purposes and elevated above the intrinsic, even the extrinsic. Some argue that the Electoral College itself devalues the intrinsic value of each citizen's vote.

Systems themselves are not bad or evil; in fact, God seems to love systems and works within organized and integrated networks! It appears that creation is placed within carefully formulated harmonious systems such as earth, our solar system, and the universe. It is people who create a system for both good and evil purposes or take an inherently good system and change the rules to benefit only a few.

It's easy to look at examples like Nazi Germany and slavery and see how unethical these systems are. However, being raised within a system can often blind us to the truth. Generally, people within a system quickly buy into the framework and become trapped in that way of thinking. Sadly, many people in modern-day America are consciously and subconsciously focused on preserving unjust practices embedded in our institutions.

Overvaluing the extrinsic

It's more challenging to see the impact of overvaluing the extrinsic because an extrinsic focus typically produces positive outcomes for the people embedded in that type of "doing." Wall Street is an example of an overemphasis on the extrinsic. The financial markets' emphasis on extrinsic outcomes, such as monetary growth, has led to the creation of an entire realm of money-making activities that are disconnected from the material economy that we all inhabit.[4]

Money is valued most in the financial system. The markets closing in 2020 at a historic high while millions of people were unemployed and a global pandemic raged on is alarming proof this is true. Wall Street is brilliant at leveraging the systemic in service of the extrinsic, but it doesn't work out so well for the intrinsic. Our elaborate financial system disproportionally supports relatively few individuals while making astronomical extrinsic gains that have nothing to do with most people on the planet.

According to the Red Book (statistics on payments and market infrastructures), published by the Bank for International Settlements, the volume of payments in the US economy is currently over $7,625 trillion, while the Gross Domestic Product (GDP) is only $21 trillion.[5] That means the monetary economy is 350 times larger than the material economy that we live and work in!

The irony in this example is that the monetary economy could also usher in unprecedented freedom and abundance if we correctly valued the intrinsic. My husband created an entire plan for this.[6] He proposes we tax the extrinsic monetary economy (payments) at a rate of 0.25% ($2.5 per $1,000) instead of taxing personal income. When we tax personal income, we are taxing the intrinsic. In his alternative plan, we could eliminate all state and federal taxes, while simultaneously

---

[4] The traditional, or "material" economy, is the world around us that we can physically see and touch. It is the economy that defines our standard of living. Examples of the material economy are the food we eat, houses we live in, cars we drive, services we use like nursing and childcare, and places we visit like malls, schools, and restaurants.

[5] The Red Book can be found here: "The Red Book statistics in a new interactive format," *Bank of International Settlements*: https://www.bis.org/.

[6] Scott Andrew Smith, *A Tale of Two Economies: A New Financial Operating System for the American Economy* (Createsoace, 2022). https://www.thefoundationforabettereconomy.org/.

ensuring that every citizen received a basic income of $2,000 each month, in addition to receiving free higher education and healthcare.

This is a compelling demonstration of how the extrinsic can serve the intrinsic. By imposing taxes on financial transactions, greater importance is placed on the intrinsic rather than the extrinsic. Additionally, the financial markets would experience a significant boost due to increased wealth in society, which would make up for any short-term financial losses caused by this new tax. Therefore, valuing the intrinsic creates a mutually beneficial scenario instead of a zero-sum one.

We are constantly confronted with an extreme focus on the extrinsic in our daily lives. Social media has perpetuated this problem with people evaluating how we look, what we do, and where we go daily. There are countless phone apps to make you look "prettier" and even put on make-up electronically, altering your external appearance. LinkedIn provides a tiny bit of space where you might write something about your intrinsic self, but it's mostly set up to display your roles, certificates, degrees, and achievements. Online dating is also largely focused on external attributes.

From a communication standpoint, think about how many emails you receive that are asking you for money. When you scroll through social media, how many posts do you see that are trying to convert your eyeballs to dollars? Since the pandemic, there's been a massive increase in online marketing, especially on LinkedIn. It used to be that one in ten of my connection requests asked me to buy something. Now it's eight in ten.

The explosion of the gig economy has only made this worse. Gone are the days when a worker could get plugged into an extensive corporate system for life. There were many benefits to working in the same place your entire career, including stability and pension-based retirements. The gig economy on the other hand puts people in a constant state of asking themselves, "Where is my next paycheck coming from?" Pension-based retirements are rapidly becoming extinct.

I find the constant barrage of extrinsic "asks" exhausting. Even philanthropic organizations are caught in this trap. I auto-donate monthly to several nonprofits, but they ask for more money every time they send me an email or mailer. They probably feel that if they stopped asking for money, they would be lost in the noise. Churches seem to feel the same way. The list goes on and on. It's a self-perpetuating system that frenetically feeds the wetiko I described in the last chapter.

Extrinsic interactions vs. intrinsic connection

Business-minded people tend to focus interactions with people on transactions: "How can this person help forward my company?" Spiritual entrepreneurs desire to shift the focus of interactions toward love. In the early days of Indigo, I tried very hard to focus on the extrinsic but quickly grew tired of the game. When I'd attend conferences or events, I wanted to consider whether or not the person I was talking to could be a future customer or investor. However, thinking in this way just wasn't me. I was so much more interested in whose energy sparked my curiosity.

For example, at a conference in San Francisco, I spent eight hours talking to one person and completely skipped the event. Laura was not someone who was going to generate money for me. She did, however, share with me circle teaching—an innovative way for training aspiring teachers.[7] She was a professor at a tiny Midwest university and espoused using co-creation circles in teaching. I had seen models of this before but not with the richness of Laura's insights.

At another conference in Reno, I only attended one session and ended up hugging the speaker and telling her I loved her afterward (we are still friends to this day). Gwen turned out to be one of the most brilliant minds on harnessing the brain to help kids learn and believe in themselves. She deeply informed my thinking on the importance of neuroscience in education. Moreover, Gwen introduced me to Greg, who brought me in to work with Native American populations, an experience that has profoundly influenced many insights in this book. Greg and I have a deep spiritual connection that transcends our mutual work in education. We would never have met if I hadn't loved a stranger in Reno.

The people I chose to focus on rarely brought immediate extrinsic benefits to my company, and they still do not in many cases. They did, however, provide incredible guidance and intrinsic motivation for me from the moment I met them, and they continue to do so even now. Real connection always has value, even if you can't measure it.

The eighteenth-century scientist and Christian mystic I wrote of earlier, Emanuel Swedenborg, says when you die, there is a life review process.[8] In that review, you see everything you've ever done, the

---

[7] Circle teaching has Native American roots. The modern method is described in the book of Christina Baldwin and Anne Linnea, *The Circle Way: A Leader in Every Chair* (San Francisco: Berrett-Koehler Publishing, 2010). I discuss co-creation circles more in chapter 5.

[8] Emmanuel Swedenborg writes, "We may also gather from this what is meant by our book of life, mentioned in the Word. It is the fact that all our deeds and all our thoughts are written on our whole person and seem as though they are read from a book when they are called out of our memory. They appear in a kind of image when our spirit is looked at in heaven's light," in *Heaven and its Wonder and Hell*, translated by George F. Dole (West Chester: Swedenborg Foundation, 2000), 463.

good and evil, but *without judgment*. It is a moment of total self-awareness. You viscerally feel the impact of each action.

Many people with near-death experiences report that during this review process, they realize that small acts of kindness and love rippled out and had more of an impact than they ever could have imagined. The currency in heaven is love and acts that grow love are of immeasurable value. The currency of a spiritual entrepreneur is also love. It is our job to refocus on valuing the intrinsic. Amazingly, this process is quite simple. You just ask yourself, does this activity, connection, or work grow love?

The intrinsic as the focus of spiritual entrepreneurship

According to Hartman, an item is intrinsically valuable if it is inherently good or beneficial in and of itself, without any negative or positive connotations attached to it. In this context, good essentially refers to the extent to which the item serves its intended function. It is easy to comprehend the concept of the intrinsic when considering the natural world. Every aspect of nature is good merely because it exists. A mountain is good because it is a mountain, and a wildflower is equally as good because it is a wildflower. It is impossible to state that one component of nature is more valuable, important, or beautiful than another.

In the Genesis story, as God was creating the world, he declared again and again that it was good. All of his creation is good.[9] Ranking and sorting is an impossible task in the realm of the intrinsic because all

---

[9] Diverse spiritual paths regard the essence of creation as an expression of God. Celtic spirituality offers a beautiful lens on the essential goodness of creation as well as the belief that what is deepest in us is the image of God. If you want to explore this from a unique lens, I recommend reading J. Philip Newell, *The Book of Creation: an Introduction to Celtic Spirituality* (Paulist Press, 1999).

things in nature are different and valuable for the very sake of existing. And all things in nature work in concert with one another as part of a more magnificent whole—our earth. *The Lion King*, the popular musical, made this concept famous in the song "The Circle of Life."
In the realm of people, it's not as easy to understand this model because we are so programmed to believe that some humans are more valuable than others. Christian platitudes such as "every person is a child of God" are meaningless without action. People sure don't act like they believe that, especially when looking back at history. Whole religions, ethnic groups, socio-economic classes, and genders have been treated as "less than" by implementing practices supported by unjust systems like slavery, racism, classism, and even genocide.

The year 2020 was one that highlighted just how far we still are from living the truth that *all* humans are made in the image of God. The video of George Floyd saying "I can't breathe" is an excruciatingly painful example of devaluing the intrinsic. The outcry across the country in protest of this horrific act reveals hope that much of society also agrees that we must refocus our systems onto the intrinsic. We have been holding our collective breaths and restricted from breathing freely largely due to systemic inequities not designed to serve all the people or each individual.

One of my favorite organizations that *does* value the individual and serve the collective is called L.O.V.E. Is The Answer.[10] The founder, A.J. Ali, started the organization in 2012 with a mission to improve police-community relations after being harassed because he was "walking while Black." In his process of producing a movie and writing a book, he realized that teaching people how to love themselves and others is truly the answer to healing everything that

---

[10] A.J. Ali, *L.O.V.E is the Answer*: trylovenow.com/.

ails individuals, communities, and nations. A.J. embodies and proclaims the spiritual entrepreneur's mission of expanding love.

I was watching *America's Got Talent* and encountered another beautiful example of an intrinsic organization—a choir named Voices of our City.[11] The choir was made up of many San Diegans experiencing homelessness. The founder, Steph Johnson, created Voices of Our City to bring hope, let the voice of the homeless be heard, and to help create pathways out of homelessness for the people in her community. As I listened to them sing, I was struck by the beauty, humanity, and love this choir embodied. The spiritual entrepreneur who created this choir embraced her work, believed in its worth, loved each member, and found humility in the process.

Whether or not you decide to start an organization like L.O.V.E. or Voices of our City, you can choose to value intrinsic organizations, businesses, and people with your dollars, time, and support.

Spiritual entrepreneurship is about people

In a similar fashion, Jesus's ministry was always about people. He met with the crowds yet saw each person as an individual. This is reflected as you read stories of Jesus's interactions and how he spoke truth—in a loving way—to each person differently. He also welcomed people who had nowhere else to go. Jesus's miracles were based on each person's humanity and worth, rather than the problems they carried. Remarkably, Jesus also performed miracles differently according to the needs and faith of each person.

---

[11] "Our Programs," *Voices of Our City*: https://www.voicesofourcity.org/.

When he healed the Centurion's servant, Jesus admired the faith of the centurion, a man from a foreign culture. When Jesus restored the blind man's sight on the Sabbath, the religious leaders around him were offended because in their eyes, he had violated the day of rest by working. When they confronted him, he reminded them that the Sabbath's purpose was to benefit people, not the other way around. This is a great example of someone confusing the intrinsic with the systemic, thinking they are being "spiritual" (intrinsic) by strictly adhering to religious tenets when they are instead valuing the systemic and devaluing the intrinsic.[12]

People were more important to Jesus than the religious perspectives that would prevent him from loving them. Jesus's miracles were unique each time: his miracles were built on personal interactions that focused on spiritual problems because he cared for the people rather than being dismayed by their shortcomings. He sought to heal the spirits and bodies of the people he encountered, loving each of them in the time they had together. Jesus is the embodiment of the intrinsic.

The path of spiritual entrepreneurs echoes the same people-centric principles. Spiritual businesses and projects often fall short from a financial standpoint despite their intrinsic value. The workers, the products, and methods seem to reject traditional business plans because the leaders aren't aiming for the traditional goals of expansion or profit. Spiritual entrepreneurs follow the paths God lays out for them, taking each opportunity as they come, always working for social betterment or change. Expanding love is always the same underlying goal, yet the paths are never the same.

---

[12] Hartman graduate student and scholar Art Ellis clarified this distinction for me and supported my exploration of Hartman's work for this book.

I consider many of the Jewish patriarchs like Abraham, Isaac, Jacob, and Joseph to be spiritual entrepreneurs. Through their stories, you can see the paths they took, how they deviated from traditions, and what happened when they followed God. Abraham left his home country on a moment's notice, a land his ancestors had lived on for generations, encountered new people, and built a family. Joseph was thrown down a well and became an advisor to the Egyptian ruler. Each path was unique and worked for the benefit of generations to come.

Spiritual entrepreneurs make use of the unique opportunities and paths God places in front of them. When A.J. was harassed by police for doing nothing besides walking, his worst nightmare transformed into a global organization inspiring millions to grow love. When Steph started Voices of Our City, she probably had no intention of auditioning for a reality TV show. Now that the choir has made national news by achieving the Golden Buzzer on *America's Got Talent*, resources, publicity, and more opportunities are available for the people the choir serves.[13]

Conclusion:
Balancing the Intrinsic, Extrinsic, and Systemic

What implications does this hold for the spiritual entrepreneur? It means that incorporating the following framework into their decision-making process will reap benefits for their businesses, customers, and communities: **Intrinsic > Extrinsic > Systemic.**

All three elements are important in running a business, and balance is the key, while always remembering that the purpose of both the

---

[13] "Voices Of The City 'Homeless' Choir Gets Terry Crews' GOLDEN BUZZER!" *YouTube*, May 27, 2020, Talent Recap, video, 4:57, https://www.youtube.com/watch?v=-tAyPwL-JCI.

systemic and extrinsic is for the benefit of the intrinsic. In the following table, I provide some business examples and questions to ask for each lens. These examples are specific to how I think about Indigo, but the table can be modified in many ways to suit any project.

Three Axiological Lenses to Assess Your Business

The Intrinsic Lens	The Extrinsic Lens	The Systemic Lens
Overall		
What are our core values?	What economic outcomes do we want to achieve?	What is our business model?
Products		
How do we want people to feel when they use our product?	Which products will most help us achieve our goals?	What systems need to be in place in order to scale?
Employees		
How do we want our employees to grow as a part of the team?	What benefits can we offer our employees?	How can we best manage our time?
Customers		
How do we honor the individual needs of each customer?	What are the company titles and roles of customers most likely to purchase?	How can we automate our processes so they are more efficient?
Marketing		
What is the intrinsic impact of our marketing?	What marketing materials do we need to produce?	Which marketing model/system do we want to use?

It's very difficult for a small company to run itself in a systematic way. Creating systems that serve people and generate extrinsic outcomes is a monumental task. When companies do figure it out, they tend to scale. Efficient systems are super important! The trap of companies as they get larger is that they often fall into serving their own systems and forget their original purpose. When this happens, the system flips from providing efficiency to creating waste and slowing innovation. The company becomes bogged down in bureaucracy.

However, that's not usually a problem for people just starting a company. The push to focus on the extrinsic is generally the challenge for a spiritual entrepreneur when starting a company, especially because funding mechanisms out there are almost 100% focused on extrinsic outcomes.

Ultimately, Jesus's words are helpful to keep in mind:

> Do not store up for yourselves treasures on earth, where moths and vermin destroy, and where thieves break in and steal. But store up for yourselves treasures in heaven, where moths and vermin do not destroy, and where thieves do not break in and steal. For where your treasure is, there your heart will be also. (Matthew 6:19-21)

When your focus is storing up treasures in heaven, it is my experience that the advice and best practices of the world no longer work. In other words, there are different rules for the road of the spiritual entrepreneur, who must focus on the intrinsic first. This is the topic of my next chapter.

Chapter 5
Rules of the Road

One of the things that has driven me crazy at Indigo is that nothing that seemed to work for other people worked for me. When I received what seemed like sound advice and followed it, it would backfire. I'd do the "right" things, but they weren't right for me. I'd hire people with a track record of success, but they were unable to repeat their success at Indigo. The techniques that worked for them in the past would not work in our context.

One expert proclaimed at the beginning of our contract that of all the companies they'd ever worked for, we were the one that held the most potential. Months later, after spending tens of thousands of dollars, they had produced no revenue, caused many tears, and walked away completely stymied. Even a well-respected marketing firm we hired early on couldn't come up with a good name for our company, a decent logo, or a succinct pitch. In the end, we hired a college kid who created our logo for $200.

For a long time, I took on all the blame for these failures. I have a history of being mean to myself internally and berating myself for "not being good enough." It took me a long time to realize that these voices weren't my own, and they certainly weren't from God either. I still struggle with my internal self-esteem. Yet, I now know that when things don't work, it is not a condemnation of me; rather, it's a reflection of how the existing system is a mismatch for my company's path spiritually. The rules of the road for spiritual entrepreneurs are completely different. External failure has no real correlation to spiritual failure. For a spiritual entrepreneur, external failure is often essential for spiritual success.

I'd like to share with you how conventional business knowledge in the following areas didn't work for me. I offer these reflections because if you're having problems in these areas, take heart! You just may be on your own spiritual entrepreneur path. The areas I'll be covering are:

1. Mentorship
2. Knowing
3. Decision Making
4. Profits
5. Pricing
6. Exits

Mentorship and Spiritual Entrepreneurship

Mentorship frequently plays an important role in entrepreneurship. Accelerators proclaim access to world-class mentors as one of the main perks for joining their programs.[1] I am blessed to have met many mentors in education and business and have often received wonderful advice.

However, the reality for me has been that while many mentors are goodhearted and well-intentioned, they often give conflicting advice. For example, one of the accelerator programs we participated in had an event called "mentor madness." There were forty mentors in the

---

[1] Startup accelerators support early-stage, growth-driven companies through education, mentorship, and financing: Ian Hathaway, "What Startup Accelerators Really Do," *Harvard Business Review*, March 01, 2016, https://hbr.org/2016/03/what-startup-accelerators-really-do.

room, and you had a couple of hours to pitch to them in groups then roam around and find the ones you wanted to talk to the most. It was fun! I loved meeting all the new people, but I frequently had two mentors who provided me with opposite advice. By the end of the night, I had gotten so much conflicting advice that it was comical. It didn't matter, though, because at this point I had already figured out how to be respectful, enjoy the person I was talking to, and take their advice with a grain of salt.

As I mentioned before, the "sound advice" that worked for other tech companies has never worked for Indigo. Eventually, I realized that the nature of mentorship and how it works in the spiritual venture realm must be different. Since the very heart of a spiritual venture involves bringing in a new way of thinking or being for humanity, there is no blueprint or template by which to do it.

I've also observed from reading the Bible that God teaches, trains, and molds his spiritual entrepreneurs in varying ways that apply to each person's unique makeup, struggles, and ancestry.[2] Since the spiritual journey is as much for the entrepreneur and those working with the entrepreneur as it is for all of humanity, each person's path will be wildly different. Therefore, any mentor with a tried-and-true approach is likely not going to be helpful.

The spiritual entrepreneur needs to have discernment, listen to the mentor's ideas without judgment, then decide for themselves what advice resonates or is relevant to their own journey. It's essential not

---

[2] Epigenetics is an emerging scientific field, defined by the CDC as the study of how your behavior and environment can cause changes in how your body reads your DNA, not in the DNA itself. Researchers are interested in epigenetics as a way to make sense of certain biological phenomena, including trauma that is passed down through the DNA for multiple generations: Matthew Tontonoz, "What Is Epigenetics, and Why Is Everyone Talking about It?" *Memorial Sloan Kettering Cancer Center*, June 19, 2018, https://www.mskcc.org/news/what-epigenetics-and-why-everyone-talking-about-it.

to get caught up in taking approaches that seem overly hyped or shallow. As a woman, I also find it necessary to discern if this advice comes from an excessively masculine perspective. Even highly successful female leaders often propose masculine tactics because it's what tends to work in standard business models. As I've said, I lead better with the more feminine aspects of flow, creativity, and co-creation.

Co-creation as a pathway forward

There is no such thing as a tried-and-true template for the evolution of humanity, as it is being co-created. Co-creation is a relatively new term in the business world. One of my favorite definitions is from the Dutch consulting firm Fronteer: "Co-creation is a form of collaborative innovation: ideas are shared and improved together, rather than kept to oneself."[3] Co-creation is the path of the spiritual entrepreneur, and remarkably, it's how God has always chosen to work with humans, walking with us on our continual process of growth. In the model of co-creation, I do believe there are mentors but rarely are they "experts." All voices are equal and valuable in the spiritual journey of an entrepreneur.

The concept of all voices being equal is an ongoing case study for me in a series of fascinating encounters. One poignant example occurred while I was in California on my way to meet a well-known personality. I had an hour break before our meeting during which I met a relatively poor, possibly homeless man in a coffee shop. He looked and sounded like the celebrity I was about to meet. His take and advice on the world were simply incredible! He viscerally showed me that diversity is part

---

[3] "What is co-creation?" *Fronteer*: https://fronteer.com/what-is-co-creation/.

of God's plan and judgment reduces our ability to see truth clearly. Nothing came of my meeting with the actual celebrity, however.

My thinking on co-creation has been deeply influenced by the Co-Active Training Institute's (CTI) coaching and leadership workshops, which utilize the following co-active coaching model.[4]

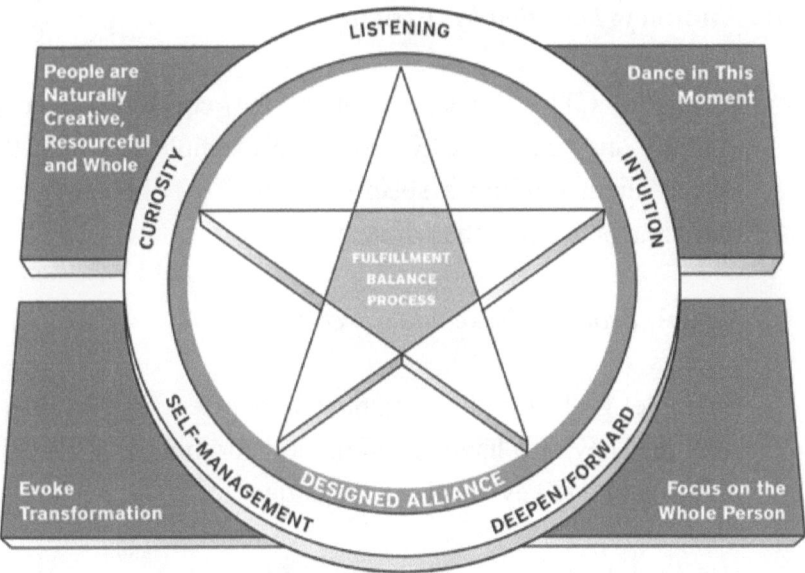

CTI's workshops are co-led by two leaders, who typically have very different perspectives and personality styles. Their core mantras are as follows:

1. People are naturally creative, resourceful, and whole
2. Nobody gets to be wrong[5]

---

[4] "What is Co-Active?" *Co-Active Training Institute*, https://coactive.com/about/what-is-coactive/

[5] CTI's "nobody gets to be wrong" principal means that the relationship between coach and client works best when you go outside of evaluation—more explicitly, removing internal judgment of yourself and the coaching client from the conversation.

If you keep these two principles in mind when working with others, the outcome will be much more powerful.

Honoring all forms of learning

CTI also addresses the three core learning styles in their workshops:

1. **Auditory**: *Learning by listening*

   Example: CTI's leaders explain the coaching concepts verbally and provide a live coaching example in which they take a client through a specific process. At the same time, participants listen to the whole process.

2. **Visual:** *Learning by seeing or reading*

   Example: CTI provides a manual with essential teachings in writing. They also have visual models for their core coaching philosophy and key coaching techniques.

3. **Kinesthetic**: *Learning by doing*

   Example: CTI has participants actively engage in practicing the coaching techniques with other participants. They also use movements, such as dance, physically jumping over a line, or walking in a particular pattern, to ground the learning within each participant's body.

CTI's diverse, interactive, and experiential teaching model for co-leadership and co-creation enables transformational learning. I've walked away from every single CTI event with a new fundamental concept that continues to live inside me on a cellular level today. When you learn something on a cellular level, you can integrate that knowledge into your mind, body, and soul simultaneously.[6]

Education, in general, needs to move to a model of co-creation that incorporates all learning styles and honors all learners as naturally creative, resourceful, and whole. What if learning weren't measured by standardized test scores but by a student's ability to develop new ways of thinking? Transformational learning would then become the norm, not the exception.

The whole idea of the "sage on the stage" persists in education because people are still looking to experts for answers. It works no better when entrepreneurs look for experts to teach them how to be successful. This approach might work when your only goal is making money, but it cannot work when your goal is to elevate human consciousness because that can only be achieved through co-creation. From this perspective, mentorship takes on a whole new level of importance and requires much more than advice to be helpful, especially for the spiritual entrepreneur. It requires what I call the co-creation circle.

The co-creation circle

A co-creation circle is a close group of friends, mentors, and allies on board for a spiritual journey. These folks are the best part of my life; they have accelerated my growth and kept me going when things got tough. When I feel completely crazy, which is often, these people help me feel sane again.

One of these co-creators, Christin Myrick, whom I quoted previously, happens to be the niece of CTI's co-founder, Karen Kimsey-House. I

---

[6] I talk more about how this works for me in the next section on "knowing."

had already been regularly involved in CTI when I met Christin and had no idea she was Karen's niece until well into our friendship. This is another example of the fascinating, unexpected connections that happen on the spiritual path. Karen deeply understands why we cannot do this work alone:

> When someone is walking beside us, we have more courage to walk into the unknown and to risk the dark and messy places in our journey.[7]

Christin and I characterize our co-creation times as church. When we both show up curious and committed, an amazing thing happens: we come up with things together that would not be possible individually. This experience makes Jesus's words "for where two or three gather in my name, there am I with them" (Matthew 18:20) feel very real and beautiful.

Many of the conclusions in this book both explicitly and implicitly mentioned came from our co-created church sessions. The pattern of co-creation happens with the people mentioned in this book and other beautiful souls not mentioned, especially the people I've worked closely with at Indigo, who are all critically important to my journey. And there will be many more that I haven't met yet. God is the constant co-creation companion of the spiritual entrepreneur, working for the good through every circumstance, talent, or flaw. This is the most comforting thought of all!

The idea of a co-creation circle isn't new. Jesus modeled this for us when he chose the twelve disciples. Jesus was showing us how to co-create the kingdom of heaven with a handful of ordinary men and a

---

[7] Karen and Henry Kimsey-House, *Co-Active Leadership: Five Ways to Lead* (Oakland: Berrett-Koehler Publishers, Inc., 2015).

few amazing women. Interestingly, Jesus chose to reveal himself first to a woman, Mary Magdalene, after he rose from the dead. Peter, James, and John were in Jesus's most inner circle, and there was a closeness and responsibility that came with that. Jesus even chose Judas to be among his disciples. So, remember, sometimes there is even a role for a Judas in our circle.

Knowing and Spiritual Entrepreneurship

The idea of "knowing" is vastly different in the world of a spiritual entrepreneur than it is in the traditional business realm. I once asked a social impact investor why he didn't feel Indigo was worthy of investment. We had revenue, proven success, hundreds of loyal customers, and a true impact focus. He said, "It's because when I ask you a question, you don't have a strong answer. You do not 'know,' you do not have a plan, and you feel uncertain to me."

I remember feeling frustrated by this investor's response because he was judging my company's worthiness, and by extension mine, based on a definition of knowing that was antithetical to the way that I experience knowing. There is the mystical definition of knowing, which refers to knowing something on an inner spiritual level.[8] This type of knowing has always made sense. Then there is the knowing of the investment world based on an egocentric conviction. Business investors like this type of conviction; they see it as confidence. Egocentric conviction, based on reciting degrees, numbers, metrics, five-year plans and goals, leaves out the most important aspects of spiritual entrepreneurship.

---

[8] See Merriam-Webster Dictionary's second definition of mysticism, "the belief that direct knowledge of God, spiritual truth, or ultimate reality can be attained through subjective experience (such as intuition or insight)," at https://www.meriam-webster.com/dictionary/mysticism.

This makes no sense to me on either the spiritual or physical level. For example, anyone who has started a company realizes quickly that plans and projections are nothing more than self-proclaimed conjectures. Typically, the "stroke of luck" that makes a company work even in a typical venture is nothing anyone could have predicted. When Google started, for example, they had no idea they would rely on ad revenue for profit. Likewise, how many companies had COVID-19 in their 2020 business plan? And yet, a founder who isn't willing to confidently project the future without flinching is so often found not worthy of investment.

This whole experience has caused me to think more deeply about knowing. What is it to "know"? Knowing from a human perspective conveys the idea of certainty, the unflinching belief that something is true or false. It's largely an activity of the mind. Scientists often project an air of certainty, but good ones know that their theories need to be adjusted or even thrown out based on new information. (And engineers always test to make sure their designs work as expected!) I once had the privilege of meeting Alan Stern, the project lead on the Pluto space mission. He said it was amazing how far off our projections about what Pluto was like proved to be when we actually visited the planet.

Mind knowing vs. cellular knowing

Mind knowing is the least powerful version of knowing. God's form of knowing is much more intimate and experiential. The first mention of "knowing" in the Bible is the idea of "knowing" in the sexual sense: "Adam knew Eve his wife, and she conceived..." (Genesis 4:1). This type of knowing is to share intimacy with another, to become one with them, to become—on a cellular level—enmeshed and transformed by that knowing. In its most holy form, something new entirely is conceived from that level of knowing.

Knowing is not really a mind thing at all in the Bible; knowing even goes beyond a heart thing. It is a mind, body, heart and soul thing and a fully immersive sensory experience that transforms you on a cellular level. Rabbi Yoel Glick describes this type of knowing as "leading to a change in perspective and a growth in awareness that is the catalyst for all spiritual evolution."[9]

This type of knowing is similar to the feeling I described earlier in this book when I first saw my husband in a crowd of 3,000 people at Mackie Auditorium. I had never met him before, but when I saw him, my entire being "knew" he was an important part of my spiritual path. Even at that level of complete cellular "knowing," I still didn't cognitively understand what this feeling meant about the future. I never would have predicted we'd be engaged three months later.

I remember when I "knew" that Indigo was part of my spiritual journey. I was on a trip in the first month of the business and I woke up in the middle of the night. Inside of me Indigo had somehow landed. It felt integrated. It was in my body somehow. I was part of Indigo and Indigo was part of me. I "knew" I was on the right track. As my husband sometimes quips, "We never really know whether we own our businesses, or whether they own us!"

How can I best describe what it is like to be a spiritual entrepreneur? The work, the journey, somehow becomes one with you, or becomes you. It's like you become more of yourself, a more refined version of yourself that leads toward intimacy with God. I don't have the words to describe the feeling. It's not even about the company anymore, or the employees, or the product: it's about the becoming, the growing, and the knowing in the deepest sense of being known.

---

[9] Rabbi Yoel Glick, "Shavuot: Touching the Infinite and Eternal," *Medium*, June 03, 2022, https://medium.com/daat-elyon/touching-the-infinite-and-eternal-6639a65a8b0d.

It seems that this is where humanity is heading. Our destiny is oneness—the concept of echad mentioned in chapter 3. The New Testament says we are to become the bride of Christ.[10] I have no idea what that really means, but the path of the spiritual entrepreneur at its core is union, not just for ourselves but for everyone, so we can know God and so our world can move forward on its path to becoming heaven on earth.

Decision Making and Spiritual Entrepreneurship

Decision-making as a CEO is something I must do every single day. I find it draining sometimes and wish that once in a while someone else could make decisions for me. I also wish that God would come down and speak with a booming voice or maybe through a burning bush and I would hear loud and clear what the answer is. That rarely happens, even in the Bible. There are a lot of aspects of decision-making that seem very different for spiritual entrepreneurs compared to traditional business practices. The aspects of decision-making that seem most different to me are:

1. Business planning
2. Saying yes
3. Saying no
4. Multi-generational focus

Decision-making: business planning

Common advice for entrepreneurship is to have a business plan, create projections, and stay focused on a task. These things are not bad; in

---

[10] Ephesians 5:22-33 describes this relationship and how it relates to earthly marriage.

fact, planning and focus are essential to running a successful business. I don't recommend that you stop organizational tasks. However, for a spiritual entrepreneur it's extremely difficult to plan in the same way conventional entrepreneurs do.

Psalm 119:105 says, "Your word is a lamp to my feet and a light to my path." If you've ever been camping or walked on a dark path at night with a flashlight or lamp, you realize it's impossible to see far ahead. A flashlight won't shine all the way to a destination or even around the next bend in the road. You must take the next step in order to see further down the path. That's how I feel the experience of a spiritual entrepreneur is. God never gives you a map of the whole path. As soon as you think you *know* where you're going, it seems to be a sure sign you are wrong.

God did appear to Moses in a burning bush and told him directly that he had been chosen to set the Israelites free. However, God did not tell Moses that it would take a season of horrific plagues, incredible pain, and people almost revolting before they could even leave Egypt. And God never said that even after becoming "free," Moses would have to face forty heartbreaking years wandering the desert dealing with rebellions, suffering, and pain, only to be refused entry into the Promised Land himself. I'm not sure Moses would have been up to the task before him if he'd known what it was really going to be like.

From that context (and so many other examples like this in the Bible), the idea of having a five-year plan, or knowing what's next on your spiritual journey or what challenges God is going to set before you and the people you lead, seems a bit ludicrous. God wants the glory, our hearts, and our absolute trust.

However, to land investments, you'll be asked to recite your five-year plan with utmost certainty over and over again. This whole concept is contradictory to the practice of following God's plan day by day, step by step, and letting go of striving to "know" the future. One of Jesus's parables is a sobering reminder of two very different types of planning:

> And he told them this parable: "The ground of a certain rich man yielded an abundant harvest. He thought to himself, 'What shall I do? I have no place to store my crops.'
>
> "Then he said, 'This is what I'll do. I will tear down my barns and build bigger ones, and there I will store my surplus grain. And I'll say to myself, "You have plenty of grain laid up for many years. Take life easy; eat, drink and be merry."'
>
> "But God said to him, 'You fool! This very night your life will be demanded from you. Then who will get what you have prepared for yourself?'
>
> "This is how it will be with whoever stores up things for themselves but is not rich toward God." (Luke 12:16-21)

Planning is another example of holding tension: planning when appropriate and being flexible at the same time. We practice the following approach at Indigo:

1. **Long-term planning:** To be honest, we do very little long-term planning at this stage of our company. Every long-term plan I've made has been changed, so it makes no sense. We do take on projects that will need more than a year to complete. For example, our IndigoPathway platform will take a total of three years to finish. Long-term projects take great amounts of focus and extreme dedication to making incremental progress each week. We set overall goals, discuss dreams, and have a wish list of future projects in our ClickUp software but hold them loosely rather than being set in our expectations. I'm not

saying long-range planning is wrong; it just hasn't worked well for us.

2. **Short-term planning:** Each week our whole team meets to review what we accomplished in the past week and to prioritize goals for the next week. This ensures we are aligned in our work and focused on the important and not always the urgent.[11]

3. **Urgent fires:** Problems, urgent requests, and unexpected snags are a constant reality in business. These must be addressed, but it's critical to not deem everything as "urgent." Making too many things urgent stresses everyone out and creates chaos. Noticing patterns in urgent requests and creating better processes and automatic responses to reduce problems are key to staying focused on what is important in business. It also provides more time to take on unexpected opportunities that appear.

4. **Unexpected blessings:** Sometimes we receive unexpected phone calls, emails, or business requests that on the surface appear to take us off track but feel clearly as the prompting of God. Our work in Mississippi (described below) and for the Navajo Nation were both catalyzed by essentially cold calls. Our entrepreneurship work started by a failed attempt to secure a grant at a foundation. A massive data project we did for the state of Colorado emerged completely out of the blue via someone I hadn't worked with in a couple years. There are hundreds of these types of encounters at Indigo, and I call them unexpected blessings. I almost always say yes when they arise.

---

[11] Steven Covey has a fantastic framework for priority management called the "Time Management Matrix" in his famous book, *The 7 Habits of Highly Effective People* (Miami: Mango Media, 2015), 202-254.

Experiences and lessons from the unexpected blessings category have profoundly shaped our work.

Decision-making: saying yes

Another key decision-making practice as a CEO is deciding which opportunities to say yes to and which to say no to. As a spiritual entrepreneur, many opportunities that you say yes to may not make any sense from a business perspective. On the other hand, I've been presented with many opportunities that sounded attractive but didn't feel right. In those cases, I either said no, or I mistakenly said yes and they fell apart anyway (all in God's grace). The outsider watching these decisions may think you a fool, unfocused, or not possessing what it takes to become a successful entrepreneur. But it could be that you just don't fit their definition of success.

As I mentioned in the "unexpected blessings" section above, the work that has been most powerful for me was completely unforeseen. I was asked to do things that I never could have imagined and often made no sense from the perspective of Indigo being profitable.

One of my favorite examples of this was a Methodist minister from Mississippi named John. John called me and said with a lovely Southern drawl, "Sheri, have you ever heard of Clarksdale, Mississippi? I'd like you to come here." Meeting the people of Clarksdale, working with their churches, nonprofits, mayor, schools, and businesses had a profound impact on my spiritual life and the way that I viewed the world.

Most of the hot button issues surrounding poverty and inequality in America were magnified in Clarksdale. And yet the people there were some of the most beautiful, brilliant, dedicated, and creative I have met anywhere in the world. We didn't solve any big problems in

Clarksdale, but it was the impetus for many things, including Vince's spiritual enterprise Lobaki—the virtual reality academy focusing on at-risk youth—coming into being.[12] John and I also continue to work on projects together and share a friendship to this day.

I said yes to John and many other random phone calls because I felt that God wanted me to say yes. So many stories and miracles came from these yeses, and so much was learned. Many of these experiences are still in progress, and there are no concrete endings yet. I feel like when people ask me about them, they are looking for some mega success story where a whole community changed or I became a "hero," but it's not like that. It's more like I played a tiny part in a much bigger, unfolding drama. We never know the full impact of our actions in our lifetimes.

Decision-making: saying no

Saying no feels more complicated to me than knowing when to say yes. I say no to emails, sales requests, and opportunities every day. If I didn't turn things down, I'd be completely overwhelmed. My assistant would probably say I need to say no more often! Overall, I say no when I feel like the energy coming from the request is not aligned with Indigo's core values. For example, if a salesperson is using marketing tricks in an attempt to manipulate me, I immediately delete their communications. If it seems a potential customer is asking for a price break or making demands out of greed and not need, we end our relationship with them. One such customer was so mad at us for having boundaries that they literally screamed at us on the phone,

---

[12] Vince, who I quoted previously, was a friend of ours in Colorado who moved to Clarksdale, in part after hearing me speak about it. This move precipitated *Lobaki.com*.

demonstrating that we definitely dodged a bullet by saying no to their business.

I also decline invitations to attend conferences that I am tempted to do out of fear of missing out or desperation. If the impetus to do something stems from a place of fear rather than a place of love, it's generally something to resist doing. As I mentioned previously, fear is a nuanced topic for spiritual entrepreneurs: it is natural to feel when doing our purpose, but fear can also divert us from our path. The question I ask myself is "what do I fear?" If I'm fearing things because of other people, it's generally a lie. If I'm afraid God won't take care of me, it is an opportunity to turn that fear into awe. Knowing the difference is embedded in the next chapter's discernment conversation.

Do not second guess your decisions

I suffer from a severe case of "woulda, coulda, shoulda," meaning I second guess my decisions far too often. When I'm doubting myself, it tends to lead to self-judgment and a lack of trust in God, which ultimately has negative consequences. Do not judge whether you made the "right" or "wrong" decision based upon a short-term outcome.[13] When God told Moses to speak to the rock to bring water out for the community, Moses instead struck it twice (Numbers 20:8-12). Water did indeed come forth, and the outcome seemed good at first. However, Moses's disobedience to God's instructions was also the reason he was not allowed to enter the Promised Land. Short-term and long-term outcomes to a decision can be very different.

---

[13] See "The Story of the Chinese Farmer" for a beautiful parable that illustrates this principle. https://conversational-leadership.net/quotation/chinese-farmer-story/.

5: Rules of the Road

If I'm honest with myself, the Moses story is scary. And yet I trust that my journey is not just about doing the "right" thing because that's not how God thinks. Truth, love, and freedom seem to be most important to God. The idea of needing an "ending" comes from our fascination with story books and movies. "Right" and "wrong" and "endings" as God sees them is something I cannot even begin to grasp. Therefore, don't seek the impact of your "yeses" and "nos" in the short term. Go with your heart and trust in the long-term outcome of God's infinite wisdom and grace.

Decision-making: multi-generational focus

Often, traditional business decision-making processes focus on accomplishment. If I make this decision, what will I get out of it? Sometimes, a founder might look at goals that are one or five years out, but typically the accomplishment is measured in a short-term time horizon. For publicly traded companies, that short-term focus is even more pronounced with quarterly earnings reports creating pressure to constantly increase numbers. Spiritual entrepreneurs are called to make decisions with an eternal perspective rather than focusing on time-bound accomplishment.

I love the Native American idea of seven generations. Their viewpoint is that when you make a decision, you make it with seven generations in mind and think about its impact over a long period of time. Oren Lyons, Faithkeeper of the Onondaga Nation, expresses this idea beautifully in the following quote:

> The Peacemaker taught us about the Seven Generations. He said, "When you sit in council for the welfare of the people, you must not think of yourself or of your family, not even of your generation." He

said, "Make your decisions on behalf of the seven generations coming, so that they may enjoy what you have today."[14]

Generations clearly matter to God. There are countless versions of genealogies recorded in the Bible. It is clear from God's conversations with Abraham that spiritual time frames are much longer than one earthly person's lifetime. As science progresses in the field of epigenetics, as well as genetics, we realize that our ancestors' life experiences, or interaction with their environment, really does matter. Researchers have now shown that trauma responses are present in the readability, or expression, of human DNA from at least six generations back and up to fourteen generations for animals.[15] Research is ongoing, but this is an example of our multi-generational impact.

It's next to impossible for humans to make decisions seven generations out. We don't know what the world is going to be like in twenty years, let alone in another couple hundred years. However, having that frame of reference in our minds elevates the conversation. Whenever you can elevate the conversation, you're getting a little closer to the viewpoint of God. God's perspective is timeless, and he sees history outside of time. When we elevate the conversation to seven generations, we're moving in the right direction. It expands our thinking to at least include the possibility of impact beyond our own lifetime.

Because of venture capital's need to exit quickly from companies, the idea of multi-generational businesses, legacy, and impact is fading from the entrepreneurial space. While legacy family businesses have their share of problems, such as trust-fund kids and tax avoidance, they

---

[14] "Seven Generations – the Role of Chief," *PBS*: https://www.pbs.org/warrior/content/timeline/opendoor/roleOfChief.html.

[14] Martha Henriques, "Can the legacy of trauma be passed down the generations?" *BBC*, March 26, 2019, https://www.bbc.com/future/article/20190326-what-is-epigenetics.

also contribute innovation and long-term vision to our economy in a way that venture capital does not. Independently owned multi-generational companies can be leveraged to improve society and change the rules of business rather than succumb to the Wall Street norms of constant growth and maximization of profit.

Folks in the climate change movement have been instrumental in getting us to think from a multi-generational perspective with the idea of not using our planet for the "here and now" but preserving it for our children and grandchildren. This multi-generational perspective also carries with it a promise. Great Lakota chief Crazy Horse said,

> I see a time of Seven Generations when all the colors of mankind will gather under the sacred tree of life and the whole earth will become one circle again. [16]

May Chief Crazy Horse's vision become reality! Spiritual entrepreneurs from all nations are working towards this vision, which also helps to transform the conversation around profit that I will discuss next.

Profits and Spiritual Entrepreneurship

Profit is a tricky topic for spiritual entrepreneurs. The reality is that money is required to operate a business, compensate staff, rent an office space, and promote an idea, product, or vision. Money is necessary, but profit is not always. That doesn't mean profit is good or bad; it simply is what it is. Profit cannot be the main goal of a spiritual enterprise. It doesn't get much clearer than Matthew 6:24:

---

[16] "Crazy Horse/Tashunca, Lakota," *California Indian Education*: https://www.californiaindianeducation.org/famous_indian_chiefs/crazy_horse/.

> No one can serve two masters. Either you will hate the one and love the other, or you will be devoted to the one and despise the other. You cannot serve both God and money.

I cannot tell you how many people have advised me, "Make your millions first, then you will have the funds, platform, and credibility to do so much more good in the world." This advice basically says to make profits your master first and then you will be better able to serve God. That is completely opposite of what Jesus is saying and defeats the whole purpose of the spiritual journey.

While it might be possible to generate huge sums of money and be a spiritual entrepreneur, my experience with folks who identify with this mission is that they only have "just enough." It seems that most often money appears on the "manna system" rather than on the stockpile system.

When I say manna, I'm referring to the Israelites wandering in the desert. God sent them manna, a sweet nutritious bread that sustained them for forty years. However, he sent them only just enough for each day. If people attempted to gather more than they could eat in one day, it would grow moldy and become inedible.[17]

A thrilling modern-day example of the manna system in action is the story of Brother Andrew in the book *God's Smuggler*.[18] Without any formal funding mechanism, Andrew was able to smuggle over one million Bibles into the former Soviet Union and communist China. Throughout the book, it is striking how God provides financial means in the most unexpected ways over many years in moments of greatest

---

[17] See Exodus 16.

[18] Brother Andrew with John and Elizabeth Sherrill, *God's Smuggler*, Expanded edition (Minneapolis: Chosen Books, 2015).

need. When he needs a car to drive the Bibles across the border, a former neighbor unexpectedly gives him a Volkswagen. When Andrew is asked to write for a Dutch magazine, even though he never asks for donations, readers of the magazine consistently send in just enough money for the work over the period of many years.

Though not as extreme as Brother Andrew, my experience at Indigo is also the manna system. We have always had just enough money come in via sales, investment, or grants to keep going. We rarely have more than three months of payroll in the bank and quite often only enough for one. It's often been a source of stress and frustration for me because I can't understand why we aren't able to convert our excellent products into more cash flow. For a long time, I searched for answers in the typical way, such as trying to mount sales campaigns or tweak our pricing, but nothing moved us from the manna model. Everyone we've brought into the company has been baffled by this issue and has tried to fix it, but none of their efforts has been successful.

It's still a source of pain because sometimes I do feel like we could have a greater impact with more money. However, I decided that I can either keep fighting the manna model or accept it. If God wants us to suddenly close million-dollar deals, it will happen. If God wants to guide me to a big investor, he will. God helped me find my husband Scott in a crowd of 3,000 when I wasn't looking for him. Why would I think that couldn't happen in business? Of course, it could. It will—if the time is ever right in God's eyes.

God did this for me so I would learn to trust him one step at a time and not trust in my own efforts or in a sum of money to see me through. Perhaps that's why he provided the Israelites with manna daily, too. It is my experience as a spiritual entrepreneur that God always provides the money we need, not the money we want. Even the Rolling Stones wrote the song "Money" about that! It is not my job to judge how much is enough. Instead, I trust God to know how much profit I need.

Pricing and Spiritual Entrepreneurship

Pricing and profit go hand in hand. Conventional advice around pricing is to charge as much as the market will bear to maximize profit. Even discount retailers offer a lower-priced product with the aim of increasing volume in order to maximize profit. Pricing is largely decided around a profit strategy.

What if pricing didn't have anything to do with profit? What if pricing were focused on maximizing real value for your customers? What if you asked yourself, "What is the right price from an intrinsic perspective?" or "What is the price that feels right for this product and service?" or "How can I maximize value for my customers at this price?"

I am criticized for not pricing my goods and services high enough, and that may be a valid point. It is difficult for me to strike the right balance between charging enough to stay in business while always making our product accessible to those who need it. I'm not an expert on pricing, so please do not try to get a pricing strategy from this book! You must do what you feel is right in your heart.

The truth is I would do everything I do for free. If I didn't have to charge, I wouldn't. One indication that your work is aligned with your purpose is that you would do it regardless of the pay, if you could. You do it because you were born to do it. When I first pitched Indigo, my opening line was,

What if people woke up every workday and thought, I can't believe they pay me to do this! That is the world we could live in if people knew who they were and were doing work that was aligned to their purpose. I want to live in a world like that.

I have always had a feeling that we work in heaven, performing jobs we love and jobs we were designed to do. That's why I was so excited to read the writings of Emanuel Swedenborg and why I was so attracted to the Church of the Holy City: it confirms this notion. He also expresses that angels feel a huge source of happiness from engaging in fulfilling jobs. He described heaven like this:

> In heaven everyone comes into his own occupation.... He comes into the employment or occupation corresponding to his use in much the same conditions of life as when he was in the world.... Yet there is this difference, that he then comes into an interior delight, because into spiritual life...and therefore more receptive of heavenly blessedness.[19]

In heaven, according to Swedenborg, all inhabitants work together in unity for the betterment of all. In hell, inhabitants work for their own gain, which contributes to the "hellish" environment.

What we do on earth corresponds to our life in the spiritual realm. And the communities we engage in with this life correspond to the communities we connect with in heaven. This is one of the key reasons I feel like people should find and do meaningful work here on earth and work with others in community. This is yet another reason why Indigo exists. If we can help more people find work that aligns with their highest purpose, we are impacting both this physical world and the spiritual one.

---

[19] Emmanuel Swedenborg, *Heaven and Hell*, Translated by John C. Ager (Start Publishing, 2012).

One of my greatest challenges with Indigo is to elevate the conversation with benefactors, students, and customers from getting a job that pays the bills to finding meaningful work. It's also a constant struggle to find customers who can pay for our products while also finding work that serves a greater purpose. We want to do both; it's just not as clear-cut as we would like it to be.

Heaven is clearly not yet fully established here on earth. Companies still need money to operate, so we have to put a price on our products and services. It doesn't mean charging to make a healthy profit is bad, or wrong. Pricing is something I struggle with personally. I'm grateful for the angst I've had around this subject because has encouraged me to delve deeper into the concept of "free". This exploration has included examining how the idea of "free" is deeply rooted in my personal upbringing, as well as how it is used as a pricing strategy in capitalist markets and considered a fundamental human right in the course of societal evolution.

"Free" as a pricing strategy

Sometimes charging a price at all seems wrong. For example, I work with a couple who provides their energy healing services at no cost because they feel like there is already an equal exchange of energy without money involved. In fact, Dave and Jody feel the work benefits them more with no financial fee for service. They feel blessed that they have the financial means to do this and realize not everyone is in a privileged position to offer services without an economic exchange. My relationship with Dave and Jody has catalyzed exponential value for me: this book would not exist without them as they introduced me to Swedenborg's work, wetiko, and many other concepts embedded in these pages.

Famous American educator Sal Khan is another example of someone who is adamant that his non-profit Khan Academy online learning videos come at no price. However, it also makes him dependent on philanthropic dollars, and he must constantly ask for donations.

The rise of freemium pricing models

On the less altruistic side of "free," the last decade has seen a rapid rise in freemium subscription-based technology models. "Freemium" combines the words free and premium. The goal is to gain market share by giving something away for free in hopes of selling a premium version to many of the users already hooked on your free product. This has worked incredibly well for many companies.

One of the best examples of a lucrative freemium model is the computer game Fortnight. The game is completely free to download and play, but you need to pay for accessories and special things your players use in the game. In 2020, Fortnite generated $5.1 billion in player spending alone (not to mention all the people making millions playing the game on YouTube).[20]

I feel like the freemium model is gaining popularity on two different levels. On one level, it's another way for companies to make money. However, on a spiritual level, I feel like humanity is moving toward this idea that a certain level of goods and services is a basic human right. The rise in acceptance of concepts like universal basic income, free college, and Medicare for all are derived from this evolution.

---

[20] Mansoor Iqbal, "Fortnite Usage and Revenue Statistics (2022)," *Business of Apps*, updated September 06, 2022, https://www.businessofapps.com/data/fortnite-statistics/.

It's critical that the rise of the freemium model really does promote more for all and doesn't get too greedy. When the system gets too greedy, it declines in value to the people using it (intrinsic), while gaining value on the stock market (extrinsic). The nature of the product feels completely different when the focus shifts from a healthy balance between profit and free towards greed.

Remember when YouTube was mostly ad-free? It was glorious. Now it's painful to watch anything on the platform since there are ads every few minutes. Did they really need the extra money? The same is true for Facebook, Instagram, and other social media platforms. When I get a few ads on social media, I don't mind, but when every other post is an ad and the platform is not showing my close friends on purpose to drive up my usage, I feel used. In fact, I am used! As they say now in the tech world: "You are the product."[21] It's exhausting. It's disheartening when services turn freemium models into money-making machines. These companies have much less value in my mind than they used to when they struck a healthier balance between delivering value and driving revenue.

My personal story of "free"

At Indigo, we recently launched a new product, IndigoPathway.com. IndigoPathway was born early-COVID when everyone in our company was laid off because schools were closed and we ran out of money. It became obvious to me that there would be millions of people out of work for a very long time who would need to pivot their careers or start their own businesses. Therefore, we created a mini version of the DISC behavioral and motivator assessments and paired those questionnaires with high-value self-awareness and career information

---

[21] Josh Klein, *You Are the Product* (St. Martin's Griffin, 2015).

results.[22] I always wanted to make the core of IndigoPathway free and use an ethical freemium model, but I received significant pushback from others with comments, such as:

- Free has no value.
- If you make it free, no one will use it.
- When you become a huge company then you can afford to make it free.
- If something is free then people will think there is some catch, some gimmick, and some way you are selling their data.

I hear these concerns and believe they are coming from a place of care. Everyone knows we have often struggled to make payroll. However, I have feelings about heavily charging for premium services, mostly because of the role "free" played in my childhood.

A world without Santa Clause

Growing up poor, free things were very important in our lives and in our ability to do things in the world. Kind people would give us free clothes, food, and gifts. I was five at our lowest point and my parents didn't have money to buy us Christmas presents. They used food stamps to get us some sweets and goodies but were disappointed that our construction paper Christmas tree, which we made ourselves, would have nothing under it.

I was a huge believer in Santa Clause and all things magical as a young child, so I was confident that as a "nice" kid, Santa would pull through. My belief was so strong that my mom felt compelled to tell me that Santa didn't actually exist so I wouldn't be deeply disappointed on

---

[22] "DISC assessment," Updated November 2022, Wikipedia, https://en.m.wikipedia.org/wiki/DISC_assessment.

Christmas morning. The effect was devastating because it eroded the fabric of my trust in my parents and in goodness.

A miracle arose from this situation that I'm only now beginning to appreciate. The local Lions Club adopted struggling families at Christmas. A jolly dressed Santa, which I now sadly knew was not real, brought us some beautiful toys and an elegant Christmas dinner. I still have the Strawberry Shortcake doll the Lions Club gave me. I loved the soft scent of her hair and breath that they somehow managed to embed into her. I used to lay awake at night snuggling that doll, comforted by her scent.

The dear, beautiful people from the Lions Club gave us something free and it still draws tears to my eyes when I think about it. It did not make us feel entitled or ungrateful or unwilling to get back on our feet. My parents worked hard to make sure other families could receive help from the Lions Club the next year. We never needed a free Christmas again.

At that time, I was unable to embrace the multiple perspectives of truth presented in that story. While the doll gave me great comfort and I loved her dearly, the memory remained a deep source of pain: pain of the loss of innocence when I realized that Santa wasn't real, pain that my parents lied to me, pain when I felt their shame and feelings of inadequacy, and shame that we were poor. But mostly, I was sad that nice kids around the world weren't getting free gifts.

Vacation Bible schools and free museum days

Recreation was expensive and my parents were creative about finding ways for us to have fun that we could afford. My summers were filled with vacation Bible schools and free museum days.

5: Rules of the Road

Mom would scour the newspaper for vacation Bible schools within an hour's radius of our house. I loved these summer camps mainly because of the free food, prizes, and crafts. I also liked learning about God, and I was a bit of a showoff. Winning competitions by knowing the most about the Bible and memorizing verses was my specialty.

One year, I was particularly obsessed with winning the grand prize, a homemade orange stuffed teddy bear about two feet high. I had already named him "Rusty" and I was in love. I've never worked so hard in my life to get something for free. Rusty is still sitting in my office at the top of my bookshelf along with many of my other special toys from childhood.

The joy of a library and free pizza

My greatest day-to-day joy growing up was also something free: the library. There was a tiny little library in Carson City, Michigan, and we were probably its most frequent visitors. I absolutely loved reading and was enthralled that you could go someplace and borrow as many books as you wanted. Reading became my escape, my adventure, my education, really. I devoured books at a breathtaking pace. I read under my desk at school when the teachers lectured. I read in the car. I read every second I could carve out of my day.

The library became even more glorious to me during the summer when you could earn free pizza just by reading. The BOOK IT! program by Pizza Hut was an unending source of joy for me. We rarely ate out and free pizza was simply too amazing to believe. When I started working in education, I heard comments by many well-meaning educators to the effect of: "It's terrible that they bribe kids to learn with prizes and free food. Kids should want to have intrinsic motivation, and you set them up to fail by enticing them with things." When I first heard a comment like this, I was horrified. That hadn't been my experience at all!

The greatest things in life really are free

I spent a considerable amount of time sharing my personal experience with the concept of free because God's forgiveness, love, and grace are all free. Our existence, our eternal life, our relationships, our value, and our purpose are all freely given to us.

This section's title is a cliché statement, but it's actually true. The things we most value, most enjoy, and most desire are all free. Essentially, everything heavenly is free. Love is the most obvious example of this. God is love, and love is the fabric of the entire universe. The very nature of love is free and promotes freedom: freedom of choice, freedom to be, to pursue dreams, to create, to sacrifice, to surrender. In his letter to the Galatian church, Paul exclaims, "It is for freedom that Christ has set us free" (Galatians 5:1). Free will is the greatest act of love and God's greatest gift to humans. I've always believed that freedom is God's most valuable gift.

The question I most ask myself as a spiritual entrepreneur is, "How can I do my work from a place of love?" In other words, how can I harness this universal love that is flowing through me and the entire universe, completely free, and allow that love to do the work, to shoulder the burden, to come up with the ideas, to propel me forward?

Pricing to maximize value

I'm not trying to avoid the pricing discussion—it's just that pricing isn't the focus. Formulas rarely work for spiritual entrepreneurs.

Pricing is a necessary evil artificially overlaid in a world where it's truly all free. I recommend that you try a lot of different price points and see what sells to the people you want to serve. Sometimes you need to charge different prices to different types of customers. Sliding scale pricing is a good example of this model. Don't focus on charging a premium price to get premium customers unless you are trying to add value to those customers. That can be a trap, taking you away from your true mission. We could have done corporate consulting at Indigo and charged ten times the price we charge schools, but then we wouldn't have had time to spend helping teachers and students.

Once you do land on a price, then ask yourself how you can deliver the most value possible to the customers who purchase your product. Setting up high-value products and services that are constantly evolving is smart business practice and integral to a spiritual enterprise.

Exits and Spiritual Entrepreneurship

The ultimate definition of success in entrepreneurship is becoming a unicorn (a company that can be sold for a billion dollars or more). Once a company becomes a unicorn, suddenly the CEO is brilliant and famous just because they hit that benchmark. Often what really happened was that a VC invested a lot of money and intentionally drove the value up, which had little to do with the CEO's leadership at all. People place so much significance on the making of money that it feeds on itself in a way that perpetuates an inequitable system and grows the insatiable hunger of wetiko.

When you think deeply enough about it, the idea of ending as a happy unicorn is rather hollow and empty. It can never be the goal of a spiritual entrepreneur. It can certainly happen but cannot be the focus.

It seems if you do receive or earn a large sum of money, you will be in danger of losing your spiritual focus and getting into the vicious cycle of wealth. Mother Teresa wrote this after she and Lynn Twist encountered a wealthy couple:

> "The vicious cycle of poverty," [Mother Theresa] said, "has been clearly articulated and is widely known. What is less obvious and goes almost completely unacknowledged is the vicious cycle of wealth. There is no recognition of the trap wealth so often is, and of the suffering of the wealthy: the loneliness, the isolation, the hardening of the heart, the hunger and the poverty of the soul that can come with the burden of wealth...You must open your heart to them and become their student and their teacher," she said in her letter. "Open your compassion and include them. This is an important part of your life's work. Do not shut them out. They also are your work."[23]

The currency of heaven is love

That story from Lynn Twist helped me to have compassion for wealthy people. So many must be painfully aware that people mainly reach out to them because they want something. Perhaps that is why they wall themselves in with the type of extrinsic funding I described previously, where it's all about exclusivity and ranking and sorting. It must be easier for them than taking a risk on the intrinsic.

The spiritual approach to investment that I have described could be incredibly freeing for wealthy funders. In the new model, they would no longer be bound to money metrics when evaluating the success of their investments. Instead, they would have the freedom to let go of

---

[23] Lynn Twist, *The Soul of Money: Reclaiming the Wealth of Our Inner Resources* (W.W. Norton & Company, 2006).

the need for a monetary return and trust in their own hearts and interest areas. It also would make it easier to get personally involved in the causes they are giving to and to form relationships with others that are not conditional.

The new measure for success could be: Does this activity, organization, or company expand love in myself and in others? Instead of striving for a monetary exit, expanding love is the goal. When we think about exits from an eternal perspective, the expansion of love is far more rewarding than temporary gain.

There are many wealthy individuals already operating this way, and beautiful examples exist throughout history. I love the story of the Milton Hershey School.[24] Milton S. Hershey, founder of Hershey's chocolate, and his wife, Catherine, shared a vision to provide a home and education for orphaned children. They were personally involved and passionate about the cause. The school has flourished and still exists today. Spiritual entrepreneurship allows funders to fully focus on the joy of giving, connecting, and loving others.

As a spiritual entrepreneur, you must find other ways to measure success, to feel good about what you're doing, and to have the courage, energy and the passion to keep moving forward. Focusing on your exit in an eternal sense can support a peaceful perspective toward success. As I mentioned at the end of chapter 4, storing up treasure in heaven is much more important (and fulfilling) than accumulating wealth on earth.

---

[24] Read more about the history of the school on their website: "About – Explore MHS History," *Milton Hershey School*: https://www.mhskids.org/about.

Conclusion: Being on the Path is Enough

I've spent many pages discussing how the rules for the road on the spiritual path might differ, summarized in the following chart:

Traditional Entrepreneurs	**Spiritual Entrepreneurs**
Mentorship	Co-Creation
Mind Knowing	Cellular Knowing
Fact-Based Decision Making	Heart-Based Decision Making
Accomplishment Focused	Multi-Generational Focused
Expanding Profit	Expanding Love
Pricing to Maximize Profit	Pricing to Maximize Value
Unicorn Exit	Eternal Exit

It's helpful to keep in mind that your road is unique, and simply being on it is enough. If you follow God's light and allow him to carry you when you are too exhausted to go on, you will not get lost, even though you will certainly feel that way many times.

While you are journeying on the road, it can be helpful to bring along a few tools to lean on. I will share some of those tools in the next chapter.

Chapter 6
Tools of the Trade

As a spiritual entrepreneur, I find various tools to be vital. Everyone possesses unique gifts from God, and certain tools may prove helpful to one individual but not necessarily to another. This chapter describes four tools that have been especially beneficial to me:

1. Prayer
2. Empathy
3. Surrender
4. Discernment

Prayer as a Business Tool for Spiritual Entrepreneurs

Prayer is *the* primary business tool of spiritual entrepreneurs. You simply can't do this work without prayer. It is your direct communication line to the spiritual realm. Prayer has more power than we can imagine.

Paul's final instructions in his letter to the church in Thessalonica emphasizes the need for continuous and praise-filled prayer:

> Rejoice always, pray continually, give thanks in all circumstances; for this is God's will for you in Christ Jesus. (1 Thessalonians 5:16-18)

I wouldn't say I'm a prayer warrior, but I do practice it every day. It's the primary way my husband and I bond. Together, we have explored many forms of prayer and found value in them all. In lieu of New Year's resolutions, I choose a yearly theme I want to focus on. Prayer was my 2020 theme. I wanted to explore different forms of prayer and grow my practice.

COVID-19 turned out to be a huge impetus for prayer personally as well as on a global scale. Our small team was hit hard early in the pandemic. All of Indigo's employees were sick in February and March, and many relatives and friends tested positive for COVID. Schools were in crisis and stopped paying their bills completely. In April, Indigo ran out of money, which had never happened before. I had to lay everyone off, including myself, and almost gave up. The manna in essence had "run out," and I felt like striking a rock like Moses did in search of water. Prayer, encouragement from my team, and support from some of our closest customers kept me going.

On top of our business woes, my husband, Scott, had a massive heart attack in August. He woke me up at midnight and collapsed on the floor saying, *"Call 911,"* but the first thing I did was grab his hand and say a five-second prayer. The heart attack was serious, with two 100% blockages in his left anterior descending (LAD) artery, known as the "widow maker." However, after undergoing a two-hour surgery and four nights in the ICU, Scott was on the road to recovery.

Like so many difficult circumstances, much good emerged from it. The heart attack catalyzed healing with Scott's family, a new chapter in our relationship, and growth in our faith. Scott rewrote his economic book with a spiritual focus, and I began writing this book. [1]

At Indigo we put most of our energies into IndigoPathway.com and added some incredible new team members with the help of the government PPP loans.[2] We built a product I'm proud of that combined the best of everything we'd learned at Indigo over the past eight years. On top of all that, Scott and I prayed more than ever!

Prayers we use regularly

This section describes several prayers that have proven to be effective for Scott and me, which we utilize for various reasons and at different times. Not all of them are strictly Christian prayers but still work beautifully in the context of Christianity. All these prayers are discussed in detail in Appendix I of this book.

1. **The Lord's Prayer**: The best example of how to pray is from Jesus himself (Matthew 6:9-13). It really covers everything! Below is the version I like best:

   > Our Father, who art in heaven,
   > Hallowed be thy Name.
   > Thy Kingdom come.
   > Thy will be done on earth, as it is in heaven.
   > Give us this day our daily bread.
   > And forgive us our sins,
   > As we forgive those that sin against us.

---

[1] Scott Smith, *The Emerging Kingdom: An Economic Guidebook to Building a Nation that is a Better Place to Live* (Independently Published, 2021). Scott's book is available on Amazon. You can learn about his economic solutions at https://www.thefoundationforabettereconomy.org/.

[2] PPP loans were part of the federal government's Paycheck Protection Program: SBA-backed loans that helped businesses keep their workforce employed during the COVID-19 crisis.

> And lead us not into temptation,
> But deliver us from evil.
> For thine is the kingdom, the power, and the glory,
> for ever and ever. Amen.

2. **Praise Prayer**: Merlin Carothers talks about this prayer in his most popular book, *Prison to Praise*.[3] It's both simple and incredibly challenging at the same time! Basically, you just praise and thank God for *everything*, especially the tough stuff.

3. **Jeanne Guyon Prayer**: Contemplative prayer is similar to meditation in that it is mainly silent. Often, a selection of scripture becomes the "mantra." The goal is to empty yourself of everything and be filled with the presence of God. It is a receiving prayer rather than an external action of talking to or requesting something from God. In her book *Experiencing the Depths of Jesus Christ,* Jeanne Guyon describes two contemplative prayer practices: "Praying the Scripture," which is pondering small portions of scripture until they become prayer, and "Beholding the Lord," which is using scripture to still your mind and then waiting quietly in God's presence. [4, 5]

4. **Ho'oponopono Prayer**: This prayer was traditionally used to resolve conflict in the Native Hawaiian culture. Both parties would ask for forgiveness in a dispute and practice the prayer before mediation. The goal was not to be "right" but to reach mutual understanding.

---

[3] Merlin Carothers, *Prison to Praise* (Escondido, CA: Merlin Carothers, 1970).

[4] Jeanne Guyon, *Experiencing the Depths of Jesus Christ* (Beaumont, TX: Seedsowers, 1975).

[5] Guyon lived from 1648-1717. Her form of prayer is the predecessor of the Centering Prayer, which Thomas Merton made famous. It's also closely related to Lectio Divina, which incorporates gospel reading, meditation, and listening all in one. https://hallow.com/blog/how-to-pray-lectio-divina/.

The four basic steps of Ho'oponopono are:

1. I'm sorry.
2. Please forgive me.
3. Thank you.
4. I love you.

We find this practice particularly helpful when we feel upset about events occurring in the world or in our relationships with others. It provides a way to participate in healing that pain by recognizing that we can ask for forgiveness for any situation due to humanity's interconnectedness. It makes Jesus's words on forgiveness feel so personal, powerful, and real.

5. **Eight-Step Prayer**: Scott learned this prayer a couple years before we got married after almost dying—that time from five blood clots in his lungs. The late Dr. Henry Wright developed this methodology to assist people in healing. Dr. Wright wrote significant works on the spiritual roots of disease.[6] Scott's version of the Eight-Step Prayer is written in detail in Appendix I. The steps are as follows:

    1. Recognize
    2. Responsibility
    3. Renounce
    4. Repent
    5. Reject
    6. Resist
    7. Restore
    8. Rejoice

---

[6] Henry W. Wright, *A More Excellent Way: Be in Health* (New Kensington: Whitaker House, 2009).

We use the Eight-Step prayer often in our relationship. It is the most powerful prayer we know for removing negative walls of emotion, *and* God used it as a way to heal my husband.

Movement prayers

In addition to more defined ways of praying such as the approaches I described above, there are many ways to pray through movement such as dancing, walking, and drumming. Thirteenth-century Sufi Muslim mystic and poet Jalaluddin Rumi started a dancing prayer practice now called whirling dervish ceremonies. Rumi told his followers, "There are many roads which lead to God. I have chosen the one of dance and music."[7]

The connection between dance, music, and spirituality is a powerful one, as many cultures have recognized throughout history. Much of the Bible was originally sung, most famously the Psalms. Indigenous cultures passed down their stories orally, often in the form of song. Penawahpskek author Sherri Mitchell summarized this perspective in her book *Sacred Instructions*:

> We are part of a uni-verse, a collection of individual notes in one continuous song; the song that sang all life into being…it exists in a vibrational frequency that emanates throughout the entire universe and resonates deep within us…As Indigenous people, we are taught to live our lives in a balanced rhythm with the harmonic frequencies that surround us.[8]

---

[7] Cara Tabachnick, "Here's what you should know before attending a whirling dervish ceremony in Turkey," *The Washington Post*, April 12, 2019, https://www.washingtonpost.com/lifestyle/travel/heres-what-you-should-know-before-attending-a-whirling-dervish-ceremony-in-turkey/.

[8] Sherri Mitchell, *Sacred Instructions: Indigenous Wisdom for Living Spirit-Based Change*, (North Atlantic Books, 2018), 5.

The idea of dancing in balance, rhythm, and harmony with God is something that resonates with many spiritual entrepreneurs. With that in mind, below are examples of movement prayers that I like:

- **Dance:** I find Nia, ecstatic dance, and the 5Rhythms dance to be especially helpful. 5Rhythms dance founder Gabrielle Roth said that the four universal healing salves are dancing, singing, storytelling, and silence.[9] She was heavily influenced by Rumi and sells some great soundtracks and videos on dance! Formalized movement practices like yoga, Tai chi, and Qigong also support prayerful mindsets.

- **Prayer beads:** Prayer beads are thought to have originated in India 3,000 years ago to enhance meditative practices.[10] They are typically called mala beads. Catholics traditionally call prayer beads a rosary. As someone who is highly distractible and needs to fidget, I find having a special string of beads is a good way to add physicality, rhythm and focus without moving a lot. You can even make your own. It seems important that the beads themselves "speak" to you. A good book on this is *A String and a Prayer: How to make and use prayer beads*.[11]

Meditation

You may have been wondering, "When is she going to talk about meditation?" Meditation is very popular right now and a powerful

---

[9] Gabrielle Roth, "5Rhythms," *5Rhythms*: https://www.5rhythms.com/.

[10] Dan Brenna, MD, "What Are Mala Beads?" *WebMD*, October 23, 2021, https://www.webmd.com/balance/what-are-mala-beads.

[11] Eleanor Wiley and Maggie Oman, *A String and a Prayer: How to make and use prayer beads* (Boston, MA: Red Wheel/Weiser, 2002).

form of prayer mentioned often in the Bible. King David is perhaps the greatest example of a Biblical leader who meditated:

> But they delight in the law of the LORD, meditating on it day and night. (Psalms 1:2)

The most basic definition of "to meditate" from the Meriam-Webster dictionary is simply "to engage in contemplation or reflection."[12] According to Healthline there are nine categories of meditation:[13]

1. Mindfulness
2. Spiritual
3. Focused
4. Movement
5. Mantra
6. Transcendental
7. Progressive relaxation
8. Loving-kindness
9. Visualization

Mindfulness meditation is the most popular in the West. The concept is derived from Buddhist teachings but is not necessarily tied to any religion. Phone apps like Headspace and Calm are great starting points for practicing mindfulness. Jeanne Guyon's form of prayer, Lectio Divina, Centering Prayer and other types of Christian contemplative practices fall in the category of spiritual meditation. We discussed movement meditation.

---

[12] *Merriam-Webster*, s.v. "Meditate," last updated October 24, 2022, https://www.merriam-webster.com/dictionary/meditate.

[13] Holly J. Bertone and Crystal Hoshaw, "Which Type of Meditation Is Right for Me?" *Healthline*, updated November 5, 2021, https://www.healthline.com/health/mental-health/types-of-meditation.

Recently, I've been practicing Jewish meditation which combines most of the categories listed above. I particularly like the incorporation of the five senses and moving those senses beyond the physical realm into the intuitive soul reality. Rabbi Yoel Glick states that "meditation empowers us to transcend our material mind-set and touch that which is Infinite and Eternal. It brings us into the living presence of God."[14] Even as a beginner, I find this to be true and invite you to try many forms of meditation and see which types support you best.

Prayer in business

Prayer is a fundamental tool of most spiritual entrepreneurs. You might not relate to any of the prayers I've listed, but it is helpful to form some sort of prayer practice that *does* resonate with you. Meditation is such an excellent prayer tool that I recommend all people have some form of meditative prayer practice even if you just start with five minutes a day. Prayer is also a gateway to growing the other tools in this chapter: praying for people helps develop empathy; discernment increases with meditative prayer; and turning things over to God in prayer is surrender.

Empathy as a Business Tool for Spiritual Entrepreneurs

My favorite definition of empathy is from Brené Brown's bestselling book, *Dare to Lead*:

> Empathy is connecting with people so we know we're not alone when we're in struggle.

---

[14] Rabbi Yoel Glick, *Living the Life of Jewish Meditation: A Comprehensive Guide to Practice and Experience*, 1st Edition (Woodstock: Jewish Lights, 2014), xvi.

Empathy is a way to connect to the emotion another person is experiencing; it doesn't require that we have experienced the same situation they are going through.[15]

It's exciting that business journals and research are recognizing empathy as a priority for innovation and retention. In 2021, research published in *Forbes* revealed empathy as the most important leadership skill.[16] The article highlighted stress and mental health, exacerbated by the pandemic, as multiplying factors in increasing the need for empathy. A global study of more than 2,000 employees by Qualitrics found 42% of people had experienced a decline in mental health during even the first few months of the pandemic in 2020. We need empathy and compassion more than ever! Empathy is one of our three core values at Indigo and a significant part of my identity.

Empaths

As I mentioned in chapter 3, I identify as an empath. An empath is simply a person who is hypersensitive to the feelings of others and the energy of the space, relationship, or connection on a deeper level than what is actually happening on a surface level. Many empaths identify as highly sensitive people, especially when they are children. One of the seminal books on empaths was written in the 1990s: *The Highly Sensitive Person*.[17] Reading that book changed my life simply through gaining the awareness that I was not alone. Most empaths state that

---

[15] Brene Brown, *Dare to Lead: Brave Work. Tough Conversations. Whole Hearts* (Vermilion: Random House, 2018). Also visit: "Dare to Lead Hub,",*Brene Brown*, https://brenebrown.com/hubs/dare-to-lead/.

[16] Tracy Brower, "Empathy Is The Most Important Leadership Skill According To Research," *Forbes*, September 19, 2021, https://www.forbes.com/sites/tracybrower/2021/09/19/empathy-is-the-most-important-leadership-skill-according-to-research/.

[17] Elaine N. Aron, *The Highly Sensitive Person* (Citadel Press, 1996). Also see "The Highly Sensitive Person," https://hsperson.com/.

just knowing they're not crazy and that there are other people like them in the world is comforting. There's another book called *The Empath's Survival Guide* that I recommend if you think you are an empath.[18]

Our first memories typically hold truths about our core self. It's often important to reexamine and choose to interpret that early memory differently than how we first interpreted the memory, especially if the memory involves trauma.

One of my early memories is of finding a baby bird that had fallen out of its nest. I desperately wanted to help this bird and begged my mother to do something. She told me that when my father came home, he would save the bird and everything would be okay. At the age of three, I was too young to comprehend that this might not be true.

While I was waiting for my father, I lay down in the dirt eye-to-eye with this baby bird. We connected in a very deep way as I witnessed its transition out of this life. When the baby bird died and the connection we shared was broken, I was devastated. I felt betrayed by my mother. I was angry with God, even though I didn't really understand the concept of God. And I was angry with my father who I thought of *as* God at the time.

I used to look back at this memory with the message that I was helpless. However, while working to process the memory, I realized that what it actually reveals is my deep sense of empathy and oneness with the world around me. When I was very young that oneness was as easy as breathing. It was a magical, all-encompassing feeling where

---

[18] Judith Orloff, *The Empath's Survival Guide* (Sounds True, 2017).

everything was possible. That connection faded quickly and was replaced with pain, shame, and powerlessness.

Many empaths experience similar disappointment growing up. Typically, there is no one to help us process our gifts, so we may shut down, become bullies, or become insecure and unable to express ourselves. This is why many empaths attract narcissists in significant relationships. And running a business in a capitalistic framework is much harder for empaths.

However, in a spiritual framework, being an empath is a superpower! I encourage young women who identify as empaths to enter the business world. I also see how the business world is starting to appreciate and see empathy as key to creating productive workplaces.

The need for empathy is a reason for including women and minorities in male-dominated industries like technology and trades. While not everyone identifies as an empath, everyone can develop and grow empathy. There are countless books on the topic and exercises to try. Even cross-cultural sensitivity training can help you develop an understanding of how others think and feel and learn to put yourself in their place. As the *Forbes* article pointed out, I view empathy as one of the great business trends of the next generation.

Empathy in business

As an empath business owner in the field of education, I feel the pain of teachers and students when I walk into schools. I also feel the pain of the people in power who are bound to a system that is debilitating and soul crushing. As someone who is sensitive to people's trauma, it's so overwhelming sometimes that I can feel paralyzed.

It took me a long time to figure out that's exactly what I was sensing when I felt troubled inside but wasn't sure what was wrong. Curiosity became one of my most powerful allies in helping to understand this better. When something comes up that is bothering me on the "people side" of Indigo, I practice becoming curious and investigating what lies at the core of a complaint, issue, or frustration. I usually find that what I initially think something is about is almost never the actual issue. Interestingly, it's often related to past trauma, both mine and theirs, trauma that is wanting to be revealed and healed. Learning that my initial assumption is almost always wrong has been a powerful lesson to slow me down and ask more questions.

One of the most difficult things about being an empath is sensitivity to what other people feel about me or my actions. In writing this book, I was concerned that people would think talking about my experiences was a means of self-promotion. Rich asked me, "Are you? Is that why you wrote the book?" I replied, "No, of course not!" Then he said, "Then why do you care what people think?" He's right. It doesn't matter what people make up about me. Jesus was labeled a glutton, a messenger of Satan, and a lunatic. How people characterized Jesus is an important lesson for the spiritual entrepreneur because it can take a lot of effort to overcome our concern about what people think of us, particularly for women and empaths.

At Indigo we measure and encourage empathy growth. It's particularly interesting when we work with people in engineering programs. Not surprisingly, empathy is not a highly valued or well-developed skill in the training of future engineers. Engineering professors have the lowest empathy scores of any education group we've ever worked with, especially the males. When we talk to them, it's not that they don't want to have empathy; in fact, it's the opposite. Many of them are dismayed, wanting to attract more women and minorities to STEM and are seeking advice to change.

They are products of a system that required them to suppress this skill to be successful. This was especially true when they were coming of age in a field that prided itself on exclusivity and ranking people out. One of Indigo's dear mentors, with a PhD in engineering, told me about his first day of undergraduate engineering school. His professor said, "Look to your left and look to your right. One of you will not be here in a year and someone within eyesight will commit suicide. If you can't hack the pressure, leave now." No wonder STEM fields are having a difficult time overcoming such a legacy!

In contrast to this, Christin Myrick, mentioned in chapter 2, is also an empath and a civil engineer and speaks often about the importance of empathy in STEM. She is well known for showing a picture of an ugly industrial waterway with concrete retaining walls contrasted with a gorgeous view of the bubbling Boulder Creek, both marvels of modern engineering. One was built with empathy and one without. Which waterway would you prefer to live next to?

> Engineering with empathy is the future. We will not survive without empathy. Engineers build our world, designing and constructing marvels. But without empathy? They are just slabs of utilitarian function. Engineers have the power to infuse compassion into every step of our design process, forward the progress of equity through the environments we build and create beauty that lasts for generations.[19]

Just as you would probably rather live next to Boulder Creek, an engineering marvel built with empathy, you might also rather do business in a world where business owners are spiritual entrepreneurs practicing empathy in their work. How amazing would it be if the

---

[19] Christin Myrick. Email to author, 2017.

dominant culture were one of people first, co-creation, and the growth of humanity?

When considering empathy as part of a spiritual enterprise I'm often thinking about the Golden Rule: Do unto others as you would want them to do to you.[20] In this way I try to be as considerate, understanding, and kind as possible. It also means constantly working on forgiving those who treat me harshly. If someone cheats me, I do my best to pray for them and do the Ho'oponopono prayer. If someone is doing wrong by our schools or kids, I do my best to send them love, asking God for healing and for good to come from the situation. Forgiving myself frequently becomes a crucial step in the process because it's common to blame myself when things go wrong.

A spiritual entrepreneur is more concerned with healing the situation rather than benefiting from it, which is totally different from normal business, which is about benefiting. It is normal for regular entrepreneurs to think of clients or competitors from the lenses of "what can I get from you" or "what can you take from me." Transactional relationships are not empathetic nor do they embrace spiritual thinking.

I've worked with a few people in business who operate with empathy, and it is beautiful. I asked a favor of one such customer and he replied, "On it, friend!" When I responded back, "Thank you, is there anything I can do for you or your school?" He said, "Just keep being you." He is such a joy to work with. Interactions like that bring nourishment to the soul and healing to the business world.

---

[20] Jesus spoke this in Matthew 7:12.

Surrender as a Business Tool for Spiritual Entrepreneurs

Surrender is such a loaded word. It conjures up different feelings and visualizations depending on the hearer. Some may think of an army, waving a white flag, giving up the battle. Others may think of it as a form of apathy or acceptance of a situation we have no control of. Surrender is a spiritual practice found in many religions and is often viewed positively. The famous proverb by Jewish king Solomon sums this sentiment up well.

> Trust in the Lord with all your heart and lean not on your own understanding; in all your ways submit [surrender] to him, and he will make your paths straight. (Proverbs 3:5-6)

Surrender can be imagined within the context of a water current. Christin and I even named the current "Amu." We've spent a lot of time exploring what it feels like in the current, how to stay in flow, how to trust her, and how to hear her. It's been fun to personify Amu and use language to make the path of surrender more accessible for our conversations. I sound so serious in most of this book, but I also find such exploration to be fun! And I'm hoping it becomes more fun so I can surrender to the current of love more fluidly.

I've always thought of my leadership path as being one of forgiveness. The more I've understood how the current works, the more it makes sense. Forgiveness is an act of letting go, an act of surrender. Christin and I have observed that forgiveness is a critical developmental task that the current demands. When we get stuck somewhere, we almost always discover that forgiveness, whether of ourselves or others, removes the obstacle preventing our journey. The Ho'oponopono prayer I've spoken of has been one of my greatest tools for practicing forgiveness.

The best description of the current that I've come across is the following excerpt from *The Book of Purpose,* a collection of teachings attributed to the legendary Jewish sage known simply as the Rebbe:

> When the Divine Light began its epic descent—a journey that conceived worlds lower and lower for endless worlds, condensing its unbounded state again and again into innumerable finite packages until focused to a fine, crystallized resolution—it did so with purpose: to bring forth a world of continuous ascent. Since that beginning, not a day has passed that does not transcend its yesterday.
>
> Like a mighty river rushing to reach its ocean, no dam can hold it back, no creature can struggle against its current. Even we, its voyageurs, cannot turn back. We must only move on with the river, on in its relentless ascent to the sea.
>
> We may appear to take a wrong turn, to lose a day in failure—it is our delusion, for we have no map to know the river's way. We see from within, but the river knows its path from Above. And to that place Above it is drawn.
>
> We are not masters of that river—not of our ultimate destiny, not of the stops along the way, not even of the direction of our travel. We did not create the river—its flow creates us. It is the blood and soul of our world, its pulse and its very fibers.
>
> Yet of one thing we have been granted mastery: Not of the journey, but of our role within it. How soon will we arrive? How complete? How fulfilled? Will we be the spectators? The props? Or will we be the heroes? [21]

---

[21] Tzvi Freeman, *The Book of Purpose: Meditation My Rebbe Taught Me* (Class One Press, 2010). Copyright and reprinted with permission of Chabad.org/7804

It is profound how in this passage, the current (the river) is ascending, as a spring appears, not descending as with earthly rivers toward the ocean. The flow is creating us and unifying us with the rest of creation. In this context, surrender is letting go of our desire to be masters of the rivers and accepting our role within it. Our role as spiritual entrepreneurs is to co-create within the flow of love.

Surrender in business

Practicing surrender as a business owner looks more like acceptance and trust rather than giving up or surrendering something. It's rooted in the belief that there is a loving God who is intimately involved in every detail of our lives, "and we know that in all things God works for the good of those who love him, who have been called according to his purpose" (Romans 8:28).

A recent personal example of surrender involved late and missing checks from the IRS and other key customers over a period of six months. If these checks had arrived on time, Indigo would have had a little buffer and some respite from the manna system. However, they never came. They were all delayed for some unexpected reason or lost in the mail; one was even deposited by accident in someone else's bank account!

Surrender didn't mean that I ignored the problem and didn't try to call the IRS or get the checks rerouted (I did!). However, it meant that I accepted this was happening for a reason and that a loving God would bring spiritual growth from the experience. It catalyzed deep conversations with several of my employees and a huge spiritual breakthrough with my husband.

The more I accepted the situation was from God and not somebody being negligent, or the IRS being inefficient, the better I felt about the situation and the more I could learn from it. Our bank account kept draining, but somehow, we always made payroll. After six months of this happening, we were finally not going to make payroll. On the last possible day, one of my team members went to pick up the mail and was so excited when he thought he saw two "checks" in there. One was a fake scam check, and the other was what looked like an IRS check but was just a letter saying they owed us money. The disappointment was compounded by the fact that this very same team member was offered over two times the salary I was paying him by a competitor that very same week. He decided to stay even in the face of possibly no paycheck. The next day the IRS check did come, and everyone got paid. I feel like the situation was so crazy that it could only be orchestrated by God.

Accepting this was God's grace and not any person's fault generated one of my greatest lessons to date. We've run out of money before, but never had I been in enough of a place of acceptance to appreciate the genius of God's love and the far-reaching impacts of everyone involved. It was a totally different experience, and I truly praised God for it. There is a big difference between going through the motions of surrender and *wanting* to believe that there is a compassionate God and feeling that truth on a cellular level over time. It inspires me to practice surrender more—I have a very long way to grow in this area.

Discernment as a Business Tool for Spiritual Entrepreneurs

Discernment is the last tool I'd like to explore. The more I learn about it, the more I realize that I've barely begun to scratch the surface on using this tool well. Because this is so critical to running a spiritual enterprise, and a lifelong skill, I feel compelled to share what I have learned.

The etymology of discernment comes from Old French *discerner*, meaning "distinguish (between), separate" (by sifting), and directly from Latin *discernere*, "to separate, set apart, divide, distribute; distinguish, perceive."[22] In her book *The Way of Discernment*, Elizabeth Leibert includes expansive definitions of discernment. Here are two that sum it up well:

> Discernment means making a discriminating choice between two or more good options, seeking the best for this moment...

> In the Christian spiritual tradition, discernment refers to the process of sifting out what is of God, discriminating between that which expresses God's call and anything that runs counter to it.[23]

Discernment vs. judgment

It's important to make a distinction between discernment and judgment. Discernment is usually what happens before we judge something. Usually, it happens so fast that we move quickly to judgment and never realize discernment and judgment are two very different things.

A wise therapist, Brenda Wentworth, helped me understand the difference between discernment and judgment.[24] She told me that the job of the ego (the mind) is never to judge. Judgment is the realm of God. Judgment is never acceptable in the realm of the human mind. This is a difficult concept for us because being created in God's image makes us prone to believe it is our right to judge.

---

[22] *Online Etymology Dictionary*, s.v. "Discernment (n.)," updated August 23, 2018, https://www.etymonline.com/word/discernment.

[23] Elizabeth Leibert, *The Way of Discernment* (Westminster John Knox Press, 2008) 8, 10.

[24] "Home," Counseling and Therapy in Boulder County, Longmont, CO, *Brenda Wentworth*: https://www.brendawentworth.com/.

This goes back to the Garden of Eden. Eve looked at the fruit and saw that it was beautiful and pleasing. She also wanted the knowledge that eating from the tree of good and evil would give her. Eve decided that her judgment of the fruit as good was truer than God's explicit commandment not to eat of the fruit. She also judged that God had been lying, as surely she wouldn't die from eating it.

Just like Eve, we are constantly deciding what is right in our own eyes; that is judgment. Discernment is not deciding whether something is good or bad, right or wrong, valuable or not valuable. Discernment is the mystical and difficult process of aligning our minds and decisions to the will of God. On a practical level, it is simply noticing what is and making a decision based on what we can impact. This type of decision-making is also a form of surrender as we explored in the last section. When you choose from a place of discernment, the mind does not dwell on what could have been, should have been, or is supposed to be. Instead, the mind accepts the will of God and is present in this immediate moment.

Getting our minds to calm down enough to even begin the process of discernment is a whole field of body and breath work that has evolved over centuries. I'll summarize my personal process next.

Breathing

Brenda also shared a key technique for preventing judgment, which involves deep belly breathing. This type of breathing is similar to what babies do instinctively. Meditation teachers espouse this practice as being helpful for spiritual growth as well as for relaxation, focus and stress reduction.

If you are new at deep belly breathing, it may be helpful to lay on the floor and put your knees at a 90° angle over something like a couch.

This allows you to breathe deeper. Now imagine that your stomach is a balloon you are blowing up by breathing in. Make sure you expand that balloon large enough so that air gets into your lower lungs, which makes your stomach rise. We don't always know where our lower lungs are, so imagine breathing to a place below your belly button or even to your feet. Ideally, that means that your diaphragm is engaging and creating a vacuum that pulls air into your lungs.[25] Breathe in through your nose. Your stomach and rib cage will expand and move outward as you breathe in through your nose and contract as you breathe out through your mouth.

When I do this just five minutes a day, it helps me to stay in discernment and recognize more quickly when I move to judgment. This is also a great prayer tool practice as breathing can be an act of prayer. After Scott and I breathe together, we generally pause another few minutes to listen and ask God for any messages and often we receive them. Listening to God is essential for spiritual discernment.

Body-based discernment

Discernment is loosely tied to the idea of intuition, another powerful tool for spiritual entrepreneurs. Many people describe intuition as a feeling in their "gut." Understanding whether a gut feeling is an instinct or a higher-level connection to God is the tricky business of discernment in itself. However, the point I want to make is that paying attention to your body can be a powerful first step on the path toward discernment. When you pay attention to sensations in your body, you become aware of the messages your body is telling you. Then you can

---

[25] Rachel Hamstra's article shares some tips on belly breathing correctly: Rachel Hamstra, "The Trouble With Belly Breathing," *Rachel Hamstra, GCFP Blog*, December 08, 2017, https://www.rachelhamstra.com/blog/2017/12/6/the-trouble-with-belly-breathing.

use those messages to help determine whether or not something is aligned with your path.

We all process incoming information with our senses, and there are different learning styles as I discussed in chapter 5. As a kinesthetic learner I process information through my body more than some. However, all of us "learn" at the body level as well as on the conscious level. Body level learning, also called "cellular learning," impacts our mind, body, heart, and soul.

In his groundbreaking book, *The Body Keeps the Score,* Dr. Bessel A. van der Kolk explores the mind-body connection—a very important part of learning, intuition and discernment—through how trauma literally reshapes both body and brain:

> Neuroscience research shows that the only way we can change the way we feel is by becoming aware of our inner experience and learning to befriend what is going inside ourselves. [26]

The mind-body connection is also a vital part of self-awareness. The next chapter outlines a self-awareness process for spiritual entrepreneurs, and body/emotion awareness is an often-overlooked part of self-awareness. My initial thoughts are often skewed when interpreting what my body is telling me. Interpreting body sensations with my mind often leads to judgment rather than discernment.

For example, I might feel sick to my stomach when I see someone and make up negative stories about them, thus avoiding that person in the future. Instead of assuming things about that person, it might be truer that I'm triggered internally by that person based on something in the

---

[26] Bessel A. van der Kolk, *The Body Keeps the Score: Brain, Mind, and Body in the Healing of Trauma* (Penguin, 2015).

past which likely has nothing to do with them. Stopping and thinking (or even praying) before reacting provides time to apply our discernment skills.

Emotional discernment

The idea that the body shares messages that can grow discernment is also true regarding emotions. *The Language of Emotions* by Karla McLaren has been most helpful to me in understanding messages emotions carry. Karla says that emotions are neither good nor bad; they are simply communicating something. Once you understand their language, you can process emotions in a healthy way that doesn't include judging, blaming, or numbing.

As an empath I feel emotions in an intensely passionate way, so much so they can often make me sick. Learning to fully feel emotions and to discern rather than make judgments about them has been integral to my journey. Emotions can be critical allies for the spiritual entrepreneur. I share Karla's sentiments below.

> Without our emotions, we can't make decisions; we can't decipher our dreams and visions; we can't set proper boundaries or behave skillfully in relationships; we can't identify our hopes or support the hopes of others; and we can't connect to, or even find, our dearest loves.[27]

Without that mind-body integration mentioned above, we often can't take the time to breathe, think, and make good decisions. Instead, we tend to react to circumstances, judge, and even lash out. We need

---

[27] Karla McLaren, *The Language of Emotions* (Boulder: Sounds True, 2010), 45.

emotions to make decisions, but emotions must be integrated with the body and the mind, not in conflict with either.

Discernment is a practice, not a destination

As a spiritual entrepreneur you may be constantly confronted with pain, emotion, judgment, and injustice. You are doing the work because you want a different world. As soon as you judge those things that cause you pain, you're becoming part of the problem. You become part of the healing by surrendering these pains over to God, trusting in him, asking for forgiveness, and sending healing energy and love.

In a recent daily devotion, Father Richard Rohr, mentioned in chapter 2, was discussing Mother Teresa. He said that while few openly criticized Mother Teresa, some suggested she should speak out more and condemn the evils and the systems that harmed the poor people she served. She said the reason she never did this was because she felt called by God to be the very embodiment of love and if she spoke out against these things, she would no longer be doing what God called her to do. We are not all called to be Mother Teresa, but she is a powerful example of focusing on what is within your control to do while letting God take care of the rest.

This does not mean you cannot speak out against injustice, nor does it mean you can't be troubled in your spirit when things are wrong. However, it does mean that you know the difference between doing what you are called to do and letting God handle the rest.

Discernment is a tricky thing because we are all wrong sometimes. We are humans, and humans, no matter how close we are to God, cannot possibly see from a big enough perspective to always get it right. Perhaps that is why God includes so many perspectives that sometimes seem contradictory in the Bible. There are two accounts of the story of David, one from the Northern Kingdom and one from Judah. Each focuses on a different aspect of the story. There are four accounts of Jesus's life, some of them leaving out parts of the plot, like his birth, that you would think every account would include. It's clear to me that God allows for diverse perspectives, and it's okay if humans don't always agree. Allowing for diversity of thought and belief is part of the process. We can never be too sure of ourselves at any time.

Discernment can also come from the Holy Spirit. There is a way to get in flow with the Holy Spirit and allow the Holy Spirit to be our main source of discernment. I've only been able to feel that occasionally. More often, I'm learning to discern between dark voices and angelic voices. I've come to realize that messages from God or angelic voices are subtle. They never push or shame. God honors our free will and never forces a decision. Dark voices on the other hand do everything in their power to make you feel like you *must* listen. They are critical, relentless, and condemning.[28] Very often they are so loud that they tend to drown out the whispers of love. Discernment involves knowing the difference between the voices in our minds.

Discernment in business

Running a business is one of the best opportunities to practice discernment daily. Business owners are faced with thousands of decisions each year from great to small, and each one, when practiced with care, is a gift for growing discernment. As I mentioned in the section on decision-making, sometimes I'm completely overwhelmed by all the decisions I must make and the repercussions of making "bad" decisions.

---

[28] C.S. Lewis, *The Screwtape Letters*, Reprint ed. (HarperOne, 2015) is a classic fictional book exploring how these "voices" speak to us.

In this effort, I keep reminding myself of two things:

1. Do not become discouraged by this struggle
2. Do not compare yourself to others

I'd suggest doing the best you can in this area and developing as much discernment as you can. Don't judge anyone who claims they talk to God and don't be too quick to believe everything they say either. I've certainly met people who claim to be hearing from the Holy Spirit, and it often seems suspect to me. This is why the Bible says to test everything you hear.[29] Remember Jesus's words:

> I am sending you out like sheep among wolves. Therefore, be as shrewd as snakes and as innocent as doves. (Matthew 10:16)

Ultimately, I've boiled down everything in my complicated relationship with discernment and decision-making to one simple question: Do I feel like I'm becoming more of my true self by choosing this path?

If the answer is yes (even if the outcome is painful in the short term), I feel like I'm discerning correctly. If the answer is no, I feel like I need to reevaluate and choose something else. I find this question is helpful not only in business, but in personal relationships, places to live, communities to join, and activities to pursue.

This question is rooted in my belief that God created our true selves to become one with him. Thus, by choosing ourselves, we are also choosing God. Choosing yes to becoming ourselves is embedded in the self-development process outlined in the next chapter.

---

[29] See 1 Thessalonians 5:21 and 1 John 4:1-6.

Conclusion: Use the Tools that Call to You

Prayer, empathy, surrender, and discernment are just four of a myriad of tools you can use as a spiritual entrepreneur. Love, non-violence, and gratitude are other tools that come to mind.[30] I encourage you to cultivate your own tools for the road of spiritual entrepreneurship.

Typically, the tools that work best for us are closely aligned to the gifts that God has endowed us with. That is why empathy, for example, is one of my greatest tools, and my greatest source of pain. Understanding who we are, how God created us, how we grow, and how we give those gifts back to others is core work of the spiritual entrepreneur.

---

[30] If you are looking for an inspiring book written by a spiritual entrepreneur that is chock full of tools, visit https://loveistheanswermovement.com as mentioned in chapter 4.

CHAPTER 7
SELF-DEVELOPMENT FOR THE SPIRITUAL ENTREPRENEUR

Since a spiritual entrepreneur's work is so closely intertwined with their life's purpose, self-development is essential. Self-development is a highly nuanced topic for me because it's also the core of Indigo. There are as many unique paths to self-knowledge as there are souls in the universe. Therefore, one-sized advice can never fit all. One path cannot be judged by another path, and we must struggle to find our own way with God.

This idea is beautifully illustrated by Jesus's final conversation with Peter in the book of John. Jesus just revealed to Peter that following him would lead to Peter's execution. (It is widely regarded that Peter was crucified upside down.) After hearing this, Peter looked over at John and wanted to know what was going to happen to him.

> [Peter] asked, "Lord, what about him?"
>
> Jesus answered, "If I want him to remain alive until I return, what is that to you? You must follow me."
>
> Because of this, the rumor spread among the believers that this disciple would not die. But Jesus did not say that he would not die; he only said, "If I want him to remain alive until I return, what is that to you?" (John 21: 20-23)

This story illustrates key pitfalls to keep in mind for the self-development journey:

- **Comparison:** It's incredibly human for us to want to know the fates of others and compare their journeys to our own journey. Comparing myself to other entrepreneurs and companies only produces suffering and prevents me from hearing God.

- **Evaluation:** Our minds are constantly evaluating others' paths and wanting to make sense of the outcomes by incorrectly assigning blame or constructing fairness narratives. Blaming myself or raging because someone harmed me in business only takes up valuable space in my heart and mind.

- **Assumptions:** We are quick to incorrectly assume a truth when trying to listen to God. If the closest believers of Jesus misinterpreted his words about John, how are we to think we would interpret God's words correctly? Many times, God has told me something via a circumstance or another person, but my assumption about the message was incorrect. Beware of trying to predict the future.

The path of others is irrelevant on our personal spiritual path. One must simply follow Jesus in the way they have been called. "Follow me," Jesus said to Peter; he says the same to each one of us. However, it's not so easy to know what "follow me" means in our daily lives.

After many years of practicing staying on the spiritual path, I've concluded that uncovering my true self—the whole self God created me to be—*is* the path. As I mentioned in the last chapter, after a big decision I ask myself, "Does this new job, relationship, church, or activity move me closer to my true self or away from it?" If the answer is "closer" (even if it feels hard), then I believe I am on the right path.

If I feel like the consequences of the decision are moving me in a direction of self that doesn't feel like me, I need to make another decision and keep moving. Author and psychologist Dr. Bill Plotkin sums this idea up beautifully:

> You need to find what is genuinely yours to offer the world before you can make it a better place. Discovering your unique gift to bring to your community is your greatest opportunity and challenge. The offering of that gift—your true self—is the most you can do to love and serve the world. And it is all the world needs.[1]

The Paradox of Self-Help

From the context that your true self is the gift you were designed to give to the world, self-awareness is critically important to the spiritual entrepreneur. It's difficult to find our true self when there is so much wounding and cultural overlay on top of who we are at a core level. Modern society also recognizes this problem and presents myriad solutions in the category of self-help. The APA Dictionary of Psychology defines self-help as "a focus on self-guided, in contrast to professionally guided, efforts to cope with life problems."[2]

There is an inordinate amount of self-help material in our bookstores and available through internet searches today. Overall, the world of self-help can be extremely useful in different stages of someone's spiritual development. I have invested a significant amount of time and resources in learning various self-help and coaching techniques, many of which have proven to be beneficial and reinforced through personal experience. In fact, at Indigo, we teach coaching techniques

---

[1] Bill Plotkin, *Soulcraft Crossing into the Mysteries of Nature and Psyche* (New World Library, 2003).
[2] *APA Dictionary of Psychology*, s.v. "self-help," https://dictionary.apa.org/self-help.

to educators. Many self-help and self-development resources are embedded in the books, websites, and articles listed in the Bibliography. Because Jesus's call to follow is individually designed, the self-development ideas in this book (or any other) may not work for you. Pursue what calls you and let the rest go.

Also, stay alert for the following two pitfalls I often see in the realm of self-help:

1. Beware that a particular self-help person or ideology does not become an idol or a religion of sorts. This happens when people judge some methods as superior to others and view followers of those methods as more evolved or spiritual. This can happen with anything from meditation to specific teachers to coaching models.

2. Beware of becoming so good at a technique that you believe you are transforming yourself, and, therefore, you have no need for God or others. The law of attraction, the prosperity gospel, and other forms of self-manifesting begin to border on this slippery slope of feeling omnipotent.[3] Thinking you *are* God is never a good thing.

The Four Stages of Self-Development

The rest of this chapter focuses on another framework developed by Dr. Robert S. Hartman.[4] This framework goes beyond self-help to self-

---

[3] See Kimberly Dawn Neumann, "What is the Law of Attraction?" Updated Oct. 17, 2022. Forbes: http://www.forbes.com/health/mind/, and Tara Isabella Burton, "The prosperity gospel explained: Why Joel Osteen believes that prayer can make you rich," September 1, 2017. Vox: https://www.vox.com/platform/amp/identies/.

[4] Robert S. Hartman, *Freedom to Live: The Robert Hartman Story*, edited by Arthur R. Ellis, 2nd ed. (Wipf and Stock, 2013), 103-125.

development. Often, the words are used interchangeably, yet there is a subtle difference in the feeling of the meaning. Self-help has a connotation that the reader is trying to fix a problem or that they aren't okay as they are. There is typically a clear goal of self-help where the person is healed or the problem is solved. Self-development has a more holistic feel to it and the idea of a continuous process of growth and discovery. In self-development, weaknesses and areas that need to be healed are identified but are also integrated into the whole person rather than seen as a deficiency.

Hartman's four-stage self-development process is an elegant way to frame the inner journey of a spiritual entrepreneur.[5]

1. Knowing yourself
2. Choosing yourself
3. Creating yourself
4. Giving yourself

These steps are constantly being cycled throughout our lives. They mirror the cycle of life, death, and resurrection, which ultimately grows love. Each step is described in the following sections.

The first stage is Know Yourself

Socrates was a big proponent of knowing yourself. "Know thyself" in Greek was etched in the Temple of Delphi. Indigo is focused on this first stage of self-development. Because our education system places so little value on the intrinsic, I find that many young people have only a vague idea as to who they are. It's probably truer to say that people

---

[5] Dr. Hartman calls these the Four Self Rules. I characterize this as a Four Stage Process for ease of reading.

have forgotten who they are. We are all born with a deep connection to ourselves, but through wounding and domestication (as Don Miguel Ruiz likes to say), the connection to ourselves weakens.[6]

Hartman says that the "first self" is about discovering:

- What kind of person you are
- What kind of properties you have
- What circumstances you were born into

There are many ways to accomplish this, and it's more difficult than it seems because so often our egos (or "small selves" as Richard Rohr puts it) are attached to a way of being or a story we made up.[7] A respected colleague asks his communication workshop attendees, "Who could you be if you didn't know who you were?" I love this idea and it brings up a good point. So much of our identity has nothing to do with who we really are.

We have no choice in almost anything that is subconsciously factored into our identity—our parents, relatives, zip code, skin color, class, neighborhood, physical appearance, height, physiology, voice, the schools we attend, and the cultural context of the time period in which we were born. The first step of knowing yourself is simply recognizing as many parts of oneself as possible and realizing that everyone has entirely different circumstances that make up their identity. Exploring both the external and internal aspects of ourselves is a worthy task.

---

[6] Don Miguel Ruiz, *The Four Agreements: A Practical Guide to Personal Freedom* (Amber-Allen Publishing, 1997).

[7] Richard Rohr describes his "small selves" concept and the search for the True Self in detail in his book *Immortal Diamond: The Search for Our True Self* (San Francisco: Jossey-Bass, 2013).

Over my life, I've found assessments particularly useful as a framework by which to look at aspects of myself in a more objective way. Indigo uses several assessments, including the Hartman Value Profile, to help people in knowing themselves.[8]

This first phase of knowing yourself can be short or can take many years; it really depends on how quickly you get to step number two, "choose yourself."

The second stage is Choose Yourself

The process of choosing yourself is based largely on Kierkegaard's work. Soren Kierkegaard was a nineteenth-century Danish philosopher who influenced existentialism and Protestant theology. One of his famous quotes is "Be that self which one truly is."[9] He believed in the power of love and in living life to the fullest.

Hartman took Kierkegaard's philosophy to mean that once you find out what kind of person you are, you have to accept yourself completely. You are who you are. Your background is your background. Your looks are your looks. Your personality and inner strengths and weaknesses are what they are. What happened to you growing up is what happened. Your experiences are your experiences. And once you choose yourself, you will be able to make the best of it.

I appreciate the concept of choosing yourself because it recognizes that as humans, we have the ability to make our own choices. To fully exercise our free will, we must first consciously choose to accept our

---

[8] Visit IndigoPathway.com if you'd like to take some of our assessments for free.

[9] "Søren Kierkegaard and the Value of Despair," October 19, 2020, *Academy of Ideas*: https://academyofideas.com/2020/10/soren-kierkegaard-value-of-despair/.

past, including our history and previous decisions. This requires us to approach our past with discernment rather than judgment. Once we've accepted our past, we can then choose to accept our present circumstances and deal with them as they are. It's important to understand that accepting our circumstances doesn't mean we're trying to control or change them. Instead, choosing to accept what *is* requires humility, which allows us to be grateful and enter into a co-creative process from where we currently stand.

There's nothing more important from the intrinsic perspective than to choose yourself. You must come to grips with the time and place and qualities with which you were born. There is an element of surrender and acceptance in choosing oneself that brings peace and trust. In this place you can begin to have gratitude for all that has happened in your life, no matter how painful. You also begin to feel forgiveness for those who have hurt you along the way and wish for them to also find peace and inner knowing.

One of the most profound personal effects of choosing myself has been a slow redefinition of fairness and justice. Most of us in the social impact space are driven by our angst that the world is not fair. There is injustice everywhere; we see it, and we want to do what we can to fix it. There is nothing inherently wrong with that idea, and most of us would never have started our journeys if we didn't feel the angst. I certainly would not have. However, when I began to choose myself, it became obvious that the mystery of our births—where, when and to whom—is inherently unfair. In the US, our zip code growing up often most determines our life outcomes, something we have absolutely no control over.

If I believe in a loving God, I must also believe that the unfairness of birth (and every tragedy that happens on earth) is somehow rooted in love. From that perspective, I have concluded that what I think is fair and what God thinks is fair are two very different things. His version of justice goes well beyond this short life. The untimely and unjust deaths of Jesus's closest followers are testaments to that truth. The shift in my thinking from choosing myself has been the greatest aid in doing my work from love rather than angst. I am not there yet; in fact, many days I feel deep despair, but the transition is in process.

As I mentioned in the last chapter, when you choose your true self, you also choose God. Your original self always was and always will be connected to the great love that connects us all. In actively choosing yourself, you are no longer separate and can now more clearly move along your path with love, rather than angst.

The third stage is Create Yourself

Some Hartman practitioners refer to the third stage of self-development as "grow yourself," but I like "create yourself" better because it conveys more freedom and expansiveness in the growing process. Kierkegaard also had a strong influence on Hartman in formulating this stage, but "create yourself" was largely inspired by ideas from Renaissance philosopher Giovanni Pico della Mirandola.

Pico was an Italian nobleman who believed that everyone should reach for their highest purpose, which was not a common belief at a time when people were not allowed direct communication with God or to aspire above their born station. He gave a famous and controversial speech, "Oration on the Dignity of Man."[10] In this speech Pico described humans as the most wondrous of God's creations because we were given the ability to reason and make choices. Moreover, our

---

[10] There are many translations of Pico's speech. Here is one resource: Giovanni Pico della Mirandola, *Oration on the Dignity of Man: A New Translation and Commentary,* ed. Francisco Borghesi, Michael Papio, and Massimo Riva. (Cambridge University Press, 2012).

choices mattered and *would* impact our destiny. Unlike animals and other forms of creation, we possess the ability to choose God's plan for our lives, or to reject it.

Creating yourself is about choosing to grow into the person God intended you to be—your true self, not just choosing to accept your circumstances. However, if you don't enter into this process without acceptance first, fully embracing the knowing yourself and choosing yourself stages, you will generally be creating a version of yourself that is not aligned with God. This is another distinction we have among all the animals—the power to create, and the power to destroy.

This process of creating ourselves happens over and over until the day we die. I suspect that we continue to create ourselves, perhaps in a new way, after we die. People who have experienced heaven in a near-death experience say that our free will and freedom increase greatly in the spiritual realm. People can imagine being with someone and instantly be transported to them or can envision a place and it will appear. They also report that we are all moving toward oneness and unity. As we move toward our true selves, it is important in the "create thyself" phase to make sure that you're not trying to create a self that other people think you should be, or a self that you feel like will be more successful, or a self that is perfect.

When you are in the process of creating yourself, you are also learning more about who you truly are. This helps you become less vulnerable to negative behaviors like comparing yourself to others, blaming yourself or others, or making incorrect assumptions about yourself or others. By gaining a deeper understanding of yourself, you can choose to be your authentic self, which is a powerful tool for personal growth and self-acceptance.

Remember, your growing self must continue to fail and learn from that failure. In a strange way, the self on this earth is somehow learning to be more human—more frail, more vulnerable, more wounded, yet more compassionate and alive. It's ironic that as we grow spiritually, it allows us to embrace our imperfections and the humanity of others more fully.

Here are three books on the self that I've found extremely helpful:

1. In ***Immortal Diamond***, Richard Rohr writes, "Life is not a matter of creating a special name for ourselves, but of uncovering the name we have always had." He describes our True Self as "that part of you that knows who you are and whose you are, although largely unconsciously."[11] Rohr defines the False Self as "just who you think you are—but thinking doesn't make it so." This book speaks beautifully to the process of self-discovery and creation from a Christ-centered perspective.

2. In ***Nature and the Human Soul***, Bill Plotkin writes, "The soul faithfully comes to our aid through dreams, deep emotion, love, the quiet voice of guidance, synchronicities, revelations, hunches, and visions, and at times through illness, nightmares, and terrors."[12] This book describes the stages of becoming more human and becoming more connected to your soul on the journey. Christin and I have referred to this book often over the past twelve years as we attempt to articulate and understand our own soul paths.

---

[11] Richard Rohr, *Immortal Diamond: The Search for Our True Self* (San Francisco: Jossey-Bass, 2013), 12.

[12] Bill Plotkin, *Nature and the Human Soul: Cultivating Wholeness and Community in a Fragmented World* (Novato: New World Library, 2008), 19.

3. In ***We are Already Whole***, Susan Gleeson writes, "I am deeply convinced that all of us, at our core, are already whole."[13] Sue feels strongly that now is the time for this idea to begin reaching society's mainstream consciousness. She provides twenty daily meditations to connect with and grow ourselves.

As you connect with your true self, you'll automatically progress towards the fourth stage of self, which involves giving back to others.

The fourth stage is Give Yourself

Hartman cited Jesus as a compelling example of someone who gave himself. While speaking with his disciples, Jesus summed this up beautifully:

> For even the Son of Man came not to be served but to serve others and to give his life as a ransom for many. (Mark 10:45)

Jesus's entire purpose on earth was to give himself and provide an example of the highest expression of human love. He gave much more than his life. Jesus gave healing, encouragement, wisdom, time, presence, prayers, connection, and most of all love.

Hartman describes the act of giving yourself in the following ways:

- Forget all limitations
- Be generous with your own self
- Give yourself to your fellow man and the world
- Love your neighbor as yourself

---

[13] Susan Gleeson, M.D., *We Are Already Whole: A Book of Reflections and Invitations* (Independently Published, 2021), 6.

Some of the ways entrepreneurs give themselves is through the process of nurturing their business, giving generously to their employees, and loving their customers. I try in every interaction to discover how I can give rather than get. Instead of pushing my own agenda with team members, I wonder, "How can I best support them right now?" When talking to a vendor or partner, I ask myself, "Is this interaction transactional or authentic?" With customers, I ask God, "How can I help them feel your love?"

The act of giving oneself is not natural. In fact, it can be draining. Done incorrectly, it can lead to burnout and even more serious issues, such as autoimmune disorders.[14] Give in proportion to your ability, knowing how much to give in each situation without draining yourself.

Energy and giving yourself

I was teaching a workshop for an education leadership group and realized how energy correlates to self-awareness. To maximize your effectiveness, at Indigo we suggest staying in the zone of your natural behaviors, motivators, and skills 80% of the time. We find this practice allows people to be more productive, comfortable, and engaged. The other 20% of the time though, we encourage people to get out of their comfort zone, adapt for others, and attempt to understand people's motivations.

This may sound a little extreme, but it capitalizes on the 80-20 rule.[15] People do their best when they are most aligned with their true self,

---

[14] I was diagnosed with Hashimoto's a couple years after starting Indigo and constantly struggle with fatigue and brain fog. Many women I know in ministry roles have also experienced autoimmune disorders. This claim is not meant to be medical or predictive in any way but from personal experience.

[15] The 80-20 rule, also known as the Pareto Principle, is an aphorism that asserts that 80% of outcomes (or outputs) result from 20% of all causes (or inputs) for any given event. In business, a goal of the 80-20 rule is to identify inputs that are potentially the most productive and make them the priority: Carla

yet people grow when they are challenged. Twenty percent may feel like a small percentage of the time, but if applied appropriately out of love and compassion, instead of out of fear and dread, the challenge can be quite effective in moving us along a more inclusive and expansive path.

From the perspective of the spiritual entrepreneur, the 80-20 rule is very true. Although it's valuable to challenge ourselves by stepping outside our comfort zones, it's equally important to align *what* we do for work, *how* we do our work, and most importantly, *why* we do our work with our God-given traits and personal calling. This ensures that we are working towards a purpose that resonates with us on a deeper level and allows us to use our unique strengths and abilities to make meaningful contributions.

We progress the fastest when we surrender to God, trust the current, and open our hearts to whatever circumstances are brought to us in each moment. Eckhart Tolle says, "wherever you are, be there totally."[16] The spiritual entrepreneur learns that we are along for the ride: we show up, do the best we can, create from whatever God sends our way, but we are not ultimately in control of what happens or doesn't happen. The outcome is for God and God alone to decide, not for us. When we choose to praise God even in the midst of difficult circumstances that we don't fully understand, and accept setbacks, grief, and pain with gratitude, we become more energized and effective. Trusting that all things work together for good for those who love God further strengthens us.

Tardi, "The 80-20 Rule (aka Pareto Principle): What It Is, How It Works," *Investopedia*, updated July 07, 2022, https://www.investopedia.com/terms/1/80-20-rule.asp. For more information, read Richard Koch, *The 80/20 Principle* (New York: Doubleday, 2008).

[16] Eckhart Tolle, *The Power of Now: A Guide to Spiritual Enlightenment* (London, England: Hodder Paperbacks, 2001).

From an energy standpoint, self-development is the key to reducing stress and building stamina through practices that fill us and bring us closer to the creator of the universe. This doesn't mean that you won't have days when you are tired, sick, or feeling unable to get out of bed in the morning. But it does mean that on those days, you don't feel so bereft; you know that in your weakness, God is strong, and you don't feel the pressure to perform or be a super person. Even God took a day to rest after creation and established the Sabbath as one of his greatest gifts to humanity.

In resting, we find strength. And in being our true selves, we get energy. Being ourselves involves clearing out the stuck energy and messages from others that we have carried with us from childhood.[17] These negative beliefs are not true and don't have anything to do with our true selves. The more energy we have, the more discernment we have, and the better we can do our work. By being clear vessels that can be filled and poured out repeatedly, we give ourselves fully to our work and to those around us. This is the essence of giving ourselves.

Loving yourself to give yourself

Loving ourselves also allows us to give more without burnout. However, the meaning of "love your neighbor as yourself" (Mark 12:31) can be distorted with egoic desires or selfish excuses. Truly loving oneself aligns with Buddhism's *metta* concept of loving-kindness. Loving-kindness implies acting with compassion toward all beings (including oneself) with an appreciation of the natural world and an awareness of the impact of our actions and non-actions. The Buddha's famous quote, "You can search the ten-fold universe and not

---

[17] There are many methods for clearing messages and stuck energy. Rick Carlson, *Taming Your Gremlin*, Revised edition (New York: Quill, 2003) is a practical book on how to do this.

find a single being more worthy of loving kindness than yourself," speaks to the idea that we are all echad (one). In an interconnected universe, loving ourselves is loving others, and loving others is loving ourselves. However, loving-kindness isn't always easy because the ego fights against acts of compassion to perpetuate the illusion of separation.

Buddha knew that his privileged upbringing was an obstacle to doing his work and freeing himself of ego, so he renounced his aristocratic life. His self-sacrifice was a form of loving himself and being generous with himself on a deeper level. This is different from the typical ways we think about loving ourselves in modern culture, which can focus on superficial needs. Sometimes we describe loving ourselves as self-care—things like bubble baths, sweet treats, and better sleep. In the proper context, these simple life pleasures are nurturing. There are also deeper layers to self-care—things like forgiveness, healing, gratitude, and reflection. All layers of self-care have value to keep ourselves healthy mentally and physically on the journey.

There are no spiritual shortcuts. We might not all have to go to such drastic measures as Buddha to follow the spiritual path, but internal work to find our true soul-self is difficult and takes time. Loving yourself, or "being generous with one's self," as Hartman puts it, is a process. You can give yourself only after knowing yourself, choosing yourself, and creating yourself. This process diminishes the impact of your small egocentric self, increasing freedom.

Conclusion: The Self-Development Model in Action for Spiritual Entrepreneurs

The amazing thing about the self-development process is that developing yourself will also develop your business. Moreover, developing a purpose-driven business will further develop yourself—a win-win situation. Below are some examples of how this can work.

1. **Self-knowing** allows spiritual entrepreneurs to know their strengths and weaknesses and delegate work accordingly to team members.

    Self-knowing at Indigo is catalyzed by personality assessments as a first step in understanding how we are different and how we are similar to other members on our team. This leads to powerful conversations that allow for more self-awareness.

2. **Self-choosing** allows spiritual entrepreneurs to choose their business just like they choose themselves—to not give up on their business when things are tough, much like they shouldn't give up on themselves.

    Self-choosing at Indigo is promoted by encouraging my team members to choose how they want to embody their role in the company and supporting that choice. For me, it's been about consciously choosing what kind of leader I want to be and accepting where I am in each stage. This is a constantly evolving process.

3. **Self-creating** allows spiritual entrepreneurs to pursue business opportunities that align with their values, vision, and self, and keeps the business genuine and able to grow exponentially as the spiritual entrepreneur and employees grow.

    Self-creating at Indigo involves accepting each circumstance that arises and choosing how we want to create from the circumstance rather than "reacting" to things that happen to us. We see challenges as opportunities for growth and successes as opportunities to celebrate. Both are great pointers, guiding us in specific directions.

4. **Self-giving** allows spiritual entrepreneurs to continue to pour themselves out for the mission of the business, nurture the people around them, and set aside their egos and need for external validation.

   Self-giving at Indigo is about supporting students, teachers and others who cross our path and need love. We give because we believe it matters, not because we think we will be compensated. Sometimes, self-giving can be difficult. There are days when we give so much that we feel a little more "reward" is deserved. However, the team learns to be content with the way things turn out. As Sueann often says, "We don't lack for love at Indigo!"

The cycle of rebirth

Self-development work is not a one-and-done process—it's a constant cycle of moving through the four stages of self from different perspectives over time. You don't leave one stage behind but integrate each experience of awareness into an ever more complete whole.

From self-knowing
To self-choosing
To self-creating
To self-giving

The spiritual journey itself is a constant cycle of rebirth.[18] Jesus talks about this in his famous conversation with Nicodemus:

> Very truly I tell you, no one can see the kingdom of God unless they are born again. (John 3:3)

Nicodemus, a learned teacher, was understandably confused by this comment, and Jesus's follow-up remarks were even more esoteric. Many people have interpreted this conversation to mean that Jesus was talking about a single point in time—when someone "gets saved." I align with the more mystical interpretation of salvation as a cycle of constantly dying to a version of oneself to experience the rebirth of a new version. This process happens over and over throughout our lifetime.

The birth canal is uncomfortable, disorienting, and downright scary! All your reference points disappear. It's like when Simone Biles pulled out of some of the 2021 Olympic events due to a phenomenon that gymnasts experience called the "twisties." Simone described it as suddenly losing her innate sense of being able to know where she was in relation to the ground at any given time. She said, "It's the craziest feeling ever…I literally cannot tell up from down"[19] I suspect this is a loss of mind-body connection. Most of her fans had compassion for her because we can relate to this happening on a personal level. It's frightening.

---

[18] The idea of life as a cycle of rebirth and non-linear time is prevalent among indigenous populations. I've gained much insight studying about the concept of the "Four Directions" from a Navajo elder. For more information visit NavajoPeople.org.

[19] Henry Austin, "What are the 'twisties?' Simone Biles explains gymnastics struggle at Tokyo Olympics," *NBC News*, July 30, 2021, https://www.nbcnews.com/news/olympics/what-are-twisties-simone-biles-explains-gymnastics-struggle-tokyo-olympics-n1275460.

I get the twisties when I'm doubting my own abilities or shaming myself. Because of my desire to grow love over profit, I'll wonder if I should have started a business at all? Maybe I should have started a non-profit? On the other hand, it's completely clear that if I did not go down the path of running a for-profit business, I never could have written this book. I've learned that the legal designation of a business is just an arbitrary overlay and doesn't really mean anything besides how you pay taxes and raise money. As I mentioned before, a spiritual enterprise can be a sole-proprietorship, non-profit, S-Corp, B-Corp, LLC, etc. These titles are simply containers—the inside heart of the business is what makes it a spiritual enterprise or not.

Going through this rebirth, the key is to embrace where you are at the moment. You can't obsess over where you were before or where you might be in the next phase of the cycle or even when you'll get there. You must be patient with yourself and give yourself the grace to be wholly immersed in the process. Writing this book, for me, while being in the middle of this cycle, was an intimidating, scary step. Who am I to give advice or speak on a subject when I'm still figuring it all out? But that is the whole point. I don't know everything, and I'm still in the process of spiritual rebirth. I always will be. *We* always will be.

We must offer what we can to the world no matter what stage we're in. Often our most painful moments give birth to something greater. This was true in the Simon Biles story. Simon inspired millions struggling with mental health. Moreover, her withdrawal from the team events provided space for her teammate MyKayla Skinner to win silver. These were greater outcomes than another gold medal. It was beautiful that we were able to witness such immediate positive outcomes from a bout of the "twisties." I love it when God makes the lessons clear for us.

Chapter 8
Revealing the Kingdom of Heaven on Earth

When I started this book, I wanted to wrap it up with a neat bow and present an amazing vision of a world replete with spiritual entrepreneurs in the future. Then I realized that wasn't really the point of the book. Instead, I want to start a conversation. My experiences as a spiritual entrepreneur, along with the many divergent topics I've addressed, are meant to be starting points for rich, deep discussions where people engage in sharing their hearts, dreams, and visions for the future. In true form to my journey, this is all I ever intended with Indigo as well. The assessments we use and workshops we lead catalyze productive conversations and help people know and value themselves and each other.

Developing self-awareness and being mindful of the spiritual journey involved in entrepreneurship can encourage more individuals to identify as spiritual entrepreneurs and move forward on their path, growing a community. Simply recognizing that this kind of engagement with business and the world is possible can shift the mindset of the industry. I hope that entrepreneurship can become a spiritual path for anyone who feels called to it, regardless of whether they believe they are deserving or lack the resources to pursue it.

The collective action of spiritual entrepreneurs and their allies can contribute to creating a world that feels like heaven on earth: a world where everyone belongs, there is enough for all, and we each have infinite value in the eyes of ourselves, each other, and God.

There are a few remaining concepts that seem relevant to creating that world, which I want to share in closing:

- Seeing with our hearts
- Growing diversity
- Driving innovation with freedom
- Collective, community-based action
- Choosing the intrinsic path

Seeing with our hearts

A new system for entrepreneurship will emerge as more founders, investors, customers, and job seekers follow their hearts and experience a mindset change around the purpose of business and their role within it. This is reflected in the following story—one that I regard as a great success moment.

I'd been working at a particular school for about three years. One of the experienced teachers there had been listening to me for a while with an odd mixture of disinterest and intrigue. He was a master at his craft and was quite strict while also being loving. This teacher was passionate about science and couldn't understand why some of his students weren't engaged. I remember when the "aha" moment hit him. He came up to me after a workshop and said,

> I finally get what you are trying to say. You are saying that I shouldn't try to change kids. I should accept them for who they are and appeal to their interests instead of forcing my own agenda. Listening to you, I suddenly realized that I wouldn't want anyone to

try to change me and I am not going do it anymore to my students. *Thank you.*

Although it may not seem significant, the moments when mindset shifts occur are what I live for. Winning the battle for a world-class education system will not happen through superior technology or better content alone, but through countless moments like the one experienced by the teacher mentioned earlier. The transformation of education will happen when educators and students not only change their perception of education intellectually but also in their hearts. The work involves creating deep connections with people, allowing them to choose a path of non-judgment and acceptance.

In the same fashion, those of us in business must also shift our minds and hearts around what matters. The Little Prince says it best: "It's quite simple: One sees clearly only with the heart. Anything essential is invisible to the eyes."[1] Seeing with our hearts is a step forward on the intrinsic path.

Growing diversity

There are a myriad of ways in which spiritual entrepreneurship will grow and be defined, and that is wonderful. I'm most excited about the spiritual capital principle of inclusivity described earlier in this book, which will open up space for a much more diverse set of spiritual entrepreneurs. A one-size-fits-all approach is no longer an option for humanity. The world is too diverse, vast, and expansive, so we should expect spiritual entrepreneurship to come in all shapes and sizes. That is why it's so critical this space doesn't become dominated by one religion, color, or socioeconomic class.

---

[1] Antoine de Saint-Exupery, *The Little Prince* (Samaira Book Publishers, 2017).

Again, this parallels my experience working in education. Our work at Indigo shows that all students are different, and a one-size-fits-all model is simply antithetical to human nature. Therefore, educational institutions must welcome more types of schools, serve all learners, measure success differently, and support diversity and variances. Almost all educators you talk to agree with this in theory, but whenever real game-changing proposals emerge onto the scene, they are usually met with bitter opposition.

The charter school movement is a prime example of this. Charter schools are free public schools. The idea behind them was to provide more choice and innovation for children. Regrettably, they have frequently been portrayed as elitist individuals who harm public education by diverting funds from the pool of money intended for public schools, thereby causing harm to other educational institutions. We work with dozens of charter schools as well as traditional public schools, and I see no evidence of such accusations being true. The charter school movement certainly drove positive change and experimentation with new models in education that we wouldn't have today without them.

In the same way, our current system of distributing the bulk of entrepreneurial money to a few within the venture capital club is robbing us of the true value that could be created by putting money in the hands of diverse spiritual entrepreneurs. This new approach to wealth distribution is based on the belief that granting more people greater freedom and choice ultimately results in beneficial innovation and growth, and it requires trust in this fundamental principle.

Driving innovation with freedom

The rise of spiritual entrepreneurship, like the charter school movement, will bring massive innovation to solving the world's most pressing problems in unique ways. To birth this level of innovation, we need to be freed from greed. When entrepreneurs are freed from the pressure of having to rapidly scale profits, or when non-profits are freed from the task of constantly raising money, they can experiment with new ways of operating, engaging communities and partnerships, leveraging technology, and using open-sourced resources. Entrepreneurship can again be the thrill of something new and creating something real and meaningful in the world, not just based on another marketing scheme or money-making formula.

Being freed from greed, also allows space for "less" being enough. Theological author Mary Ford Grabowsky beautifully explains the freedom of "less":

> Freedom is about choices: Freedom to choose less rather than more. It's about choosing time for people and ideas and self-growth rather than for maintenance and guarding and possessing and cleaning. Simple living is about moving through life rather lightly, delighting in the plain and the subtle. It is about poetry and dance, song and art, music and grace. It is about optimism and humor, gratitude and appreciation. It is about embracing life with wide-open arms. It's about living and giving with no strings attached.[2]

With the principle of enoughness we discussed earlier in the book, spiritual entrepreneurs can choose to be free of the need to scale and maximize profit, allowing them to give with no strings attached. It doesn't mean you have to take a vow of poverty like St. Francis of Asssi or Mother Theresa did (though you certainly could), but it means you hold the tension of being in this world and yet connected to God, our source of eternal unconditional love. Perhaps by choosing

---

[2] Mary Ford-Grabowsky, ed., *Sacred Voices: Essential Women's Wisdom through the Ages* (San Francisco: HarperOne, 2002), 209–210.

freedom, as the Israelites did, walking through the miraculous splitting of the Red Sea, you might find a way with God that no one has ever heard of before.[3]

Like the charter school movement, if we restrict this emerging field with preconceived notions, old-fashioned standards, or fear of letting the old system die, we will reduce freedom. More than that, we reduce the possibility of the miraculous, the supernatural, and all that is truly amazing about being a spiritual entrepreneur. Freedom is essential for any system to work, and love is the foundation for freedom. That is why God honors free will and allows us to choose a path outside of love.

Collective, community-based action

The movement of spiritual entrepreneurship will not emerge by funding new billion-dollar unicorns or in attempting to become a hero by solving a global problem individually. It will emerge through many people collectively working as a community, sharing resources, and growing together.

The encouraging thing is that your community probably already has members who have come up with brilliant solutions to every one of its most pressing problems. Likely, some are already implementing these solutions in small ways with success. However, they aren't the people in power, nor do they have resources to grow.

When I consult at schools, there are always a few master teachers and students with specific solutions to improve their schools. They also

---

[3] The Lubavitcher Rebbe discusses this idea in an anthology of talks. See Rabbi Menachem M. Schneerson, *Likkutei Sichot*, Volume 3, 969, *Chabad*: https://www.chabad.org.

understand the unique context of their school and community, considering the challenges that prevent these solutions from being implemented. Their perspectives are essential to sustainable and equitable change. However, these grass root voices are rarely valued or empowered.

Finding these overlooked problem solvers and equipping them with the right team, capital, and tools to do the job locally (without the pressure to scale) is a powerful approach to community development. There are latent spiritual entrepreneurs in every community I've met with, and every time I meet them, I'm always inspired. Relying on existing systems mired in old ways of thinking will only perpetuate the problem no matter how much lip service they provide otherwise. Typically, existing organizations with access to substantial capital are not interested in change because their power and capital are often dependent upon the existing system staying in place. It's rare that a large organizational player will undergo the mindset shifts necessary to implement substantive change on its own.

True shifts are created by choosing the intrinsic and by remembering echad—we are one—each connected to God and to each other. In this sense, we are all participating in revealing the kingdom of love together. Spiritual entrepreneurship is a collective community working together to expand love. Expanding love happens every day when people have moments of awareness, which produce new ways of thinking, and positive actions.

Choosing the intrinsic path

If you do choose to follow the intrinsic path, there will be times when you want to turn back. It is a strange feeling and at first you won't be quite sure what you've chosen. The path you were on before may seem easier and more familiar. This is because the usual paths are more formulaic. They offer a clear game plan that you can win with: there are maps to follow that produce predictable outcomes. This dilemma reminds me of Jesus's words (which are often misinterpreted):

> Enter through the narrow gate. For wide is the gate and broad is the way that leads to destruction, and many enter through it. But small is the gate and narrow the way that leads to life, and only a few find it. (Matthew 7:13-14)

After traveling the intrinsic path for a while, you get to a point in the journey where you feel like Neo in *The Matrix*.[4] You finally took the "red pill," your whole reality shifts, and there is no turning back. Suddenly, the future feels more uncertain than ever, *and* you have been rendered unable to operate in the conventional framework of business. This state can be confusing and frustrating all at the same time, but it's worth it!

Only after taking the red pill and choosing the path of faith can you explore your full potential and the full impact of accessing love at its source: the love that binds us all, the love that never fails, the love that carries each one of us when we feel like we cannot go on as we wander in the desert.

Conclusion: The Kingdom of Heaven is Among Us

The kingdom of heaven has been growing like a mustard seed (Luke 13:18-19) ever since the presence of Jesus on earth two thousand years ago, if not for millions of years before then. Despite the despair and suffering still on our planet, humanity *is* moving toward unity, justice, love, and peace. We can all choose whether we will show up, live our

---

[4] *The Matrix*, directed by Lana Wachowski and Lilly Wachowski (United States: Warner Bros, 1999).

purpose, and embark on the intrinsic journey. I agree with Charles Eisenstein, author of *Sacred Economics*, who believes that we are in a crucial point in history where the world is rapidly changing with seemingly opposite realities emerging at the same time.

> We are in a time of tremendous volatility, not just externally, but for many people internally as well. On a daily basis, it seems, the world is flipping from one timeline to another to another. The future looks dark; I blink my eyes and all is bright. A blue sky fills with clouds in a minute, then they are gone again. Multiple realities coexist on a single planet. Multiple realities coexist in a single person.[5]

Eisenstein's sentiments capture the roller coaster that many of us feel in our deepest core. The world is changing in fundamental ways, and sometimes it is hard to know whether we are going backward or forward as multiple realities converge in the global and national geopolitical landscape. It is my core belief that humanity is in the process of taking a monumental leap forward into a new level of consciousness, and we are experiencing the birthing pains of bringing about this new consciousness. It is this collective shift in consciousness that is the underlying root cause of the angst and dissatisfaction that so many employees are currently feeling, as well as many students as they contemplate entering the workforce.

Spiritual entrepreneurs are a critical part of revealing the "blue sky" reality that Eisenstein describes. This is a people-centered world in which economics *can* be sacred and God's principles of inclusivity, enoughness, and intrinsic value are the norm and not the exception.

---

[5] Charles Eisenstein, "Volatility," *Charles Eisenstein* (blog), January 23, 2022, https://charleseisenstein.substack.com/p/volatility?s=r.

Expanding love in liminal space

It is essential that we become comfortable with and learn to thrive in liminal space. Liminal is from the Latin word *limen*, which means threshold. A liminal space is the time between "what was" and "next." It is a place of transition, a time of waiting and not knowing the future.[6] Liminal space is the norm on the path of a spiritual entrepreneur because the nature of doing something tangible in the world, while maintaining a spiritual focus, requires constant transformation.

While speaking on a panel for aspiring entrepreneurs, someone asked, "How do you grow as leaders?" All the other panelists had concrete answers with books to read, classes to take, etc. I said, "If you are doing the work, the work will grow you." Since love is the fundamental energy of the universe, aiming to expand love grows us—not just ourselves personally, but everyone and everything around us.

Liminal space is not meant to be controlled but to be surrendered to. You must let go of everything completely. When you encounter anything challenging, you must meet and embrace it purely and completely as a gift from God. If it is light, then receive it and let it shine from within you. If it is dark, then forgive it and trust that God will provide a way forward (again, the Ho'oponopono prayer is one of the best ways to do this).

The irony is the process of surrendering to the constant transformation of liminal space can feel like anxiety and scarcity while conjuring up feelings that you are not enough. The process of expanding love doesn't feel romantic, cozy, or comfortable. That is because liminal

---

[6] "What is a Liminal Space?" *In A Liminal Space*: https://www.inaliminalspace.org/about-us/what-is-a-liminal-space. See also Kimberly Dawn Neumann, "Liminal Space: What Is It and How Does It Affect Your Mental Health?" *Forbes*: https://www.forbes.com/health/mind/.

space is meant to be transitory and transformational. In fact, the human experience on earth is liminal.

In addition to our own fears, we can't help but feel the anxiety of the collective—the whole human system. It can be overwhelming, even panic inducing, replete with feelings of dread and immobility. I've found it is important to ask myself, "What part is actually mine and what is coming from elsewhere?" Sometimes the fear is coming from bigger external energies happening in the world, and sometimes fear is coming from my own past unresolved trauma. Just realizing this lessens the pressure and stress.

Wherever the fear or suffering comes from, the work is to heal or repair it—not on our own, or through our efforts, but with the assistance of divine love and grace. The idea of repairing the world is represented in Judiasm by the term *tikkun olam*. Tikkun olam encourages us to contribute to the common good, thus repairing the world and revealing the kingdom of heaven. "We need to repair the world so that its Creator is no longer hidden within, but shines through each thing in magnificent, harmonious beauty."[7] The process of healing is the same as I shared earlier: recognize and apologize for the suffering, forgive it, release it to God, and infuse the collective with love and appreciation.

The energy must move. It is only when you stop moving that it feels like fear and death. The challenge is that to move the energy, you must be still and know there is a God (Psalm 46:10). In other words, you must slow down in present time to go forward. You can't see where you're going until you see where you are and where *we* are as a

---

[7] Tzvi Freeman, "What Is Tikkun Olam? What does Tikkun Olam mean, who came up with it, and how do I do it?" *Chabad Org*, June 15, 2017, https://www.chabad.org/library/article_cdo/aid/3700275/jewish/What-Is-Tikkun-Olam.htm.

community. We can't rely on our own limited vision but must seek to see through heaven's eyes.

Look at your life through heaven's eyes

In the spirit of holding many truths at once, remember while this *is* about you and your path, it's also *not* about you at all. The spiritual entrepreneur plays their part in the great tapestry of God's Kingdom. I'll leave you with Jethro's song to Moses from *The Prince of Egypt*. May you look at your life through heaven's eyes.

> A single thread in a tapestry
> Though its color brightly shines
> Can never see its purpose
> In the pattern of the grand design
>
> And the stone that sits on the very top
> Of the mountain's mighty face
> Does it think it's more important
> Than the stones that form the base?
>
> So how can you see what your life is worth
> Or where your value lies?
> You can never see through the eyes of man
> You must look at your life
> Look at your life through heaven's eyes. [8]

---

[8] "Through Heaven's Eyes," *The Prince of Egypt* (DreamWorks, 1998).

Appendix I
Discussion Questions

These discussion questions are designed to facilitate heartfelt conversations. They can be answered on your own but more effectively with a group of others striving toward the same goals.

In the Jewish tradition, a group of like-minded individuals discussing deeper meaning in the scriptures is called a *havurah*.[1] When a group comes together with no "right" answer in mind and a sincere desire to learn together, amazing insights emerge.

Reading this book while also referring to whatever scriptural texts and prayers that align with your faith will greatly enhance the meaning. Finding meaning in connection with others is a worthy effort. Most of the learning garnered on my journey as a spiritual entrepreneur as well as my personal spiritual journey has been forged in the context of relationships.

---

[1] Many resources on *havurah* and the layers of meaning in scripture exist. For an excellent overview that relates to Western Christians, I recommend listening to Marty Solomon and Brent Billings, "Jewish Hermeneutics," March 28, 2019, in *BEMA Discipleship Podcast Episode 110*, podcast, MP3 Audio, https://www.bemadiscipleship.com/110.

Discussion suggestions for Chapter 1:
The Backstory to This Book

Goal: To help you understand how your spiritual context shaped your path and the multiple perspectives you hold.

1. What is your spiritual context?

2. Five-minute life story activity: Take a blank piece of paper. Draw your life timeline from birth until now. Make a note of high and lows, events that stand out to you and help tell the overarching theme of your personal story. This will look like a jagged line across your page (like a stock market graph). Look for patterns. Use this visual guide to share your story with others in your group in five minutes or less.

3. What "winner" or "victim" perspectives have you taken for granted as truth? Are there personal stories or historical moments you'd like to explore from another perspective?

4. Share an example of a tension of two opposite truths you struggle to hold in your life.

Discussion suggestions for Chapter 2:
The Three Dimensions of Spiritual Entrepreneurship

Goal: To identify as a spiritual entrepreneur or identify people you know who are spiritual entrepreneurs, and what that might practically mean in your life or in their lives.

1. How has your work helped you grow spiritually?

2. Which people in your life do you identify as fellow travelers on your spiritual journey? If you have employees, how do you think of them and what does your relationship with them look and feel like?

3. How do you use both masculine and feminine energies in your work? Do you favor one or the other?

4. In what ways are you already engaged in elevating human consciousness?

5. How do you define the kingdom of heaven? What do you imagine it looks, feels, sounds, and smells like?

6. What part of that new world do you feel called to bring into reality?

Discussion suggestions for Chapter 3:
The Three Principles of Venture Capital

Goal: To discuss how the principles of venture capital have impacted you personally even if you haven't raised money. And to think about how you or others might invest differently.

1. What experiences have you had with investment that have been both positive and painful?

2. What types of new investment strategies, models, or organizations would you like to see for spiritual entrepreneurs?

3. How do you rank and sort yourself internally? Where do you feel like your value stems from?

4. Which exclusive "clubs" have you tried to enter (or entered)? How did it feel?

5. If you were investing in an organization and didn't use money as a measure at all, how would you define success?

6. What are some examples of investors who have chosen a different path for investment?

Discussion suggestions for Chapter 4:
Valuing the Intrinsic

Goal: To integrate the Hartman model and provide your own context for understanding it. And to think about value in your own life.

1. Can you give an example where you overvalued the intrinsic, extrinsic, or systemic dimensions?

2. Which of Hartman's dimensions do you default to and why?

3. What do you value most?

4. How do you define your own value?

5. If you were part of changing the conversation around "value" in one area, which would it be?

6. Create a Hartman dimension lens chart for your own business or life and explore how the dimensions of intrinsic, extrinsic, and systemic relate to key areas of your business or personal life. See the chart on page 102 "Three Axiological Lenses to Access Your Business."

Discussion suggestions for Chapter 5:
Rules of the Road

Goal: To discuss the points brought up in this chapter and think about how parts of the chapter relate in your life or business.

1. How do you *"know"* something?

2. Who is in your co-creation circle and why?

3. What is your personal decision-making framework?

4. How does profit play a role in the larger goal of your business?

5. What does an exit mean to you and how do you define an exit from a spiritual context?

Discussion suggestions for Chapter 6: Tools of the Trade

Goal: To reflect on the tools discussed in the chapter as well as explore and share other tools you personally use.

1. Do you identify as an empath? If so, how do you typically view this trait? If not, do you know someone who might be an empath that you can have a conversation with?

2. What is your current prayer practice? Are there other prayers that you relate to and can share with others?

3. How do you feel about discernment? Are there techniques you use to discern whether an idea is coming from God or not?

4. When you think about surrender, what images come to mind? Do you relate to the idea of a current, or water? Is there something that would be helpful to surrender in your life right now?

5. What other tools do you use on your personal and professional spiritual journey? Can you teach one of these tools to someone in your life right now?

Discussion suggestions for Chapter 7:
Self-Development for the Spiritual Entrepreneur

Goal: To reflect on your self-development journey and actively engage in the process.

1. In what ways have you gained self-awareness? Can you share tools or experiences that supported you in this process?

2. Do you feel like you have accepted or chosen who you are? What are some areas where you feel like you might still be resisting choosing yourself?

3. How do you like to grow and create yourself? Can you think of an example of growing that brought you closer to your true self and God?

4. How do you currently give yourself? Is the way you are choosing to give yourself causing stress or sickness? Are there ways you can give yourself more or practice self-care more?

5. Are there different self-development models or frameworks you feel are helpful and support your spiritual growth?

Discussion suggestions for Chapter 8:
Revealing the Kingdom of Heaven on Earth

Goal: To envision being part of the spiritual entrepreneurship movement and support those on the path.

1. What role do you feel like God is asking you to fill in revealing the kingdom of heaven or in repairing the world?

2. Imagine a world where spiritual entrepreneurship is the dominant model for business. What would that look like and feel like? How would it change your life?

3. What communities are you part of now? How can you get more involved and/or share this message with them? What do you want to build together?

4. What do you love most? How does that translate into your work?

5. How do you feel about liminal space? Are there ways in which you can recognize it or become more comfortable with it over time?

6. Do a short meditation or listen to the song from *The Prince of Egypt*. If you looked at your life through heaven's eyes how would your current perspective change?

Appendix II
Descriptions of the Prayers

This section describes each prayer mentioned in chapter 6 and what they mean personally, while providing some tips on how to pray them. Prayer is different for everyone, and all faith paths have beautiful prayer traditions to experience. Therefore, feel free to try these yourself or discover other prayers that resonate.

The following prayers are included:

1. The Lord's Prayer
2. Praise Prayer
3. Jeanne Guyon Prayer
4. Ho'oponopono Prayer
5. The Eight-Step Prayer

The Lord's Prayer

The best example of how to pray is from Jesus himself! The Lord's prayer is incredibly powerful on many levels. It makes sense why many churches say it every week. Below is the translation that I like best (Matthew 6:9-13):

> Our Father, who art in heaven,
> Hallowed be thy Name.
> Thy kingdom come.
> Thy will be done on earth, as it is in heaven.
> Give us this day our daily bread.
> And forgive us our sins,
> As we forgive those who sin against us.
> And lead us not into temptation,
> But deliver us from evil:
> For thine is the kingdom, and the power, and the glory,
> For ever and ever. Amen.

The Lord's prayer directly relates to the spiritual entrepreneur's journey and connects to the other prayers mentioned in this book.

- "Our Father, who art in heaven, hallowed be thy Name" acknowledges that there is a God and that we can intimately connect with God on earth. One way to cultivate a close relationship with our Creator is by practicing Jean Guyon's method of prayer, which involves simply enjoying the presence of the Holy One.

- "Thy Kingdom come. Thy will be done on earth, as it is in heaven" is the overall aim of the spiritual entrepreneur.

- "Give us this day our daily bread" is the concept of manna as we discussed in chapter 5. Jesus prays for daily bread, not a storehouse of bread.

- "As we forgive those who sin against us" reflects the constant practice of humanity for increasing love. Jesus showed us this path by forgiving those who crucified him. "Father, forgive them; for they know not what they do" (Luke 23:34) is one of the most powerful statements ever made.[1] The Ho'oponopono prayer is an effective way to practice forgiveness.

- "But deliver us from evil" is something we all need. The Eight-Step prayer is a great way to practice casting evil from our presence and turning to God for healing.

- Giving God "the power and the glory forever and ever" reminds us to stay humble and praise him for all things that occur. The Praise Prayer is a beautiful reminder of that.

Praise Prayer

Merlin Carothers talks about the praise prayer in his famous book *Prison to Praise*.[2] His books have sold over nineteen million copies, yet very few people have ever heard of him. Carothers's basic principle of praising and thanking God for everything, especially tough stuff, is difficult to wrap our minds around. His book was an absolute game changer for me. He describes this process as "spiritual dynamite."

---

[1] Jesus said this while hanging on the cross to the people who had just crucified him.

[2] I recommend this book as a must read for spiritual entrepreneurs who identify as Christians. It's short but powerful.

> I have come to believe that the prayer of praise is the highest form of communion with God, and one that always releases a great deal of power into our lives. Praising Him is not something we do because we feel good; rather it is an act of obedience. Often the prayer of praise is done in sheer teeth-gritting willpower; yet when we persist in it, somehow the power of God is released into us and into the situation. At first in a trickle perhaps, but later in a growing stream that finally floods us and washes away the old hurts and scars.

I'm still in the teeth-gritting stage of practicing this prayer. When I *can* praise God in the face of adversity, the results do seem to be miraculous. I would love to get to the place in my heart where I truly do thank God at all times and for every detail of my life.

Well before Merlin wrote *Prison to Praise*, the ten Boom sisters practiced this prayer in one of the most horrible places on earth: a Nazi concentration camp. Their story is extraordinary and almost every page of Corrie ten Boom's book *The Hiding Place* beautifully illustrates the praise prayer in action. My favorite story involves fleas.

After months of imprisonment elsewhere, Betsy and Corrie found themselves in the death camp Ravensbruck. They finally made it to the barracks and were discouraged that their situation had gone from bad to worse. Moreover, they were assaulted by fleas. Corrie was horrified, exclaiming, "Betsie, how can we live in such a place?" Betsie replied by asking God to "show us how" and quoted the scripture: "Rejoice always, pray constantly, give thanks in all circumstances; for this is the will of God in Christ Jesus." (1 Thessalonians 5:16-18).

Corrie and Betsy then proceeded to praise God for every single thing in the new foul-aired barracks, including the fleas (much to Corrie's dismay). Later, it was revealed that the fleas were the reason why the guards did not go into the barracks, leaving the prisoners alone to conduct Bible studies and talk freely among themselves.[3] The praise prayer is simple but powerful! Try it.

Jeanne Guyon's Prayer

A man once told me that my destiny is to become an apostle, not an activist. When I asked him what that meant or how I could possibly become an apostle, he told me to read *Experiencing the Depths of Jesus Christ* by Jeanne Guyon. Like so many seminal spiritual texts, I was surprised that this book was not more well-known in the Christian world.

Madame Jeanne Guyon was a French Catholic mystic who lived from 1648-1717. She was thrown into the Bastille for her teachings on how to pray by surrendering herself to the presence of God. This type of prayer, known as "praying the scripture" or "beholding the Lord," is similar to meditation with scripture being a mantra. The goal is to empty yourself of everything and be filled with the presence of God. Guyon explains the way of praying like this:

> Whatever truth [scripture] you have chosen, read only a small portion of it, endeavoring to taste and digest it, to extract the essence and substance thereof, and proceed no farther while any savor or relish remains in the passage: when this subsides, pick up your book again and proceed as before, seldom reading more than half a page at a time, for it is not the quantity that is read, but the manner of reading, that yields us profit.

---

[3] Corrie ten Boom, Elizabeth Sherrill and John Sherrill, *The Hiding Place,* 35th ed., 209-210. Another excellent book with powerful perspectives on the Holocaust and gratitude in the face of adversity is Viktor Frankl, *Man's Search for Meaning* (Boston: Beacon Press, 2006).

When I read Madame Guyon's book, and especially her autobiography, it's very hard for me to imagine what it's like to be so completely enmeshed with God the way Jeanne and many of the mystics were. Experiencing suffering, such as when she was thrown into the Bastille or contracted smallpox, brought her joy. She was living the praise prayer centuries before Merlin Carothers. Guyon wanted for nothing in this life except to be in communion with Jesus Christ. I included this prayer in the book because it's important, not because I'm good at it!

Guyon's manner of praying was a predecessor of the Centering Prayer, which Thomas Merton made famous. Lectio Divina is another type of contemplative prayer that can support the process of learning to experience God's presence in this way.

Ho'oponopono Prayer

The Ho'oponopono prayer was traditionally used to resolve conflict in the Native Hawaiian culture. Both parties would ask for forgiveness in a dispute and practice the prayer before the confrontation. The goal was not to be "right" but to reach mutual understanding.

Imagine if before you started to fight with your significant other, you went through the steps both mentally and verbally and in your heart, "I'm sorry, please forgive me, I appreciate you, and I love you." Our fights would go a lot differently if we took that approach.

Ho'oponopono has evolved significantly over time and was made famous in Western culture by the book *Zero Limits* by Dr. Hew Len.[4]

---

[4] Joe Vitale and Ihaleakala Hew Len, *Zero Limits: The Secret Hawaiian System for Wealth, Health, Peace, and More*, 1st ed. (Wiley, 2009).

In his book, Dr. Len describes his use of Ho'oponopono in his work with patients in a psychiatric prison. Patients were helped by his prayers, some dramatically, even though he was not able to see many of them in person. Scott and I find the practice very helpful, especially when keeping Christ and his forgiveness in the picture.

When I find myself judging something, being angry at institutional injustice or someone that really bothers me, I do the Ho'oponopono prayer for them, that injustice, or that pain. It could be me suffering, or it could be the teachers and students I serve; both instances serve as opportunities to use this prayer. This is something I *can* do and it's much more helpful than judgment. It keeps me in the discerning realm.

The beauty of this prayer is that in the act of bearing witness to the suffering, it is in a sense also my suffering. Because we are all interconnected, I see my own complicity in the pain and can help heal it by forgiving it and asking for forgiveness myself. I'm a novice in truly understating this mystery, but Richard Rohr explains this well:

> "Resurrected" people are the ones who have found a better way by prayerfully bearing witness against injustice and evil—while also agreeing compassionately to hold their own complicity in that same evil. It is not over there—it is here. It is our problem, not theirs. The Risen Christ, not accidentally, still carries the wounds in his hands and side. The question becomes: How can I know the greater truth, work through the anger, and still be a life-giving presence?[5]

Practicing Ho'oponopono is a beautiful way to work through the anger and still be a life-giving presence. The steps are as follows:

---

[5] Richard Rohr, "The Zealots and the Pharisees," July 12, 2022, *Center for Action and Contemplation*: https://cac.org/daily-meditations/the-zealots-and-the-pharisees-2022-07-12/.

Step 1: Repentance, "I'm Sorry"

The first step is simply being sorry. It doesn't even have to be something you did. You can be sorry for any pain or suffering you encounter in the world. The energy healers I mention in this book, who introduced me to this prayer, say that as soon as you encounter suffering, it is yours. It has been given to you so that you might offer help, healing, and forgiveness. Often, I pray things like:

- I'm sorry I'm feeling judgmental towards this person.

- I'm so sorry there is so much pain in the education system.

- I'm sorry that I feel jealous toward this person with more financial resources than I have.

By saying you are sorry, you are taking responsibility for this issue in your life or in the world around you. You feel remorse and sadness that this exists in yourself and in humanity.

Step 2: Ask forgiveness, "Please Forgive Me"

Asking forgiveness is a powerful way to heal our own pain and the pain of the world around us. Jesus bookends the Lord's Prayer with an emphasis on the importance of forgiveness:

> For if you forgive other people when they sin against you, your heavenly Father will also forgive you. But if you do not forgive others their sins, your Father will not forgive your sins. (Matthew 6:14-15)

I struggle with the exact interpretation of this scripture, but it is clear that forgiveness has far reaching implications in the spiritual realm.

The way I apply this scripture to my work is to pursue a leadership model of forgiveness. When I feel offended, cheated, in pain, depressed, or weary, I do my best to practice Ho'oponopono. Sometimes when I'm frustrated to my wits' end with humanity, my heart simply echoes Jesus's prayer on the cross, "Father forgive them, they know not what they do" (Luke 23:34).

As a leader, my primary job is to forgive and take responsibility for myself and the suffering I feel around me. In the context of my examples in step one, here is how I might continue the prayer:

- Please forgive me for my judgment. Please forgive me for trying to be you and for all the pain judgment causes in the world.

- Please forgive me for contributing to the pain in the education system. Forgive my ancestors who also contributed to that pain. Forgive all those who consciously and unconsciously create pain. Forgive those who take that pain on themselves and judge their self-worth based on the pain that isn't theirs.

- Forgive me for comparing myself to others and for becoming jealous. Forgive me for not feeling secure in your love. Forgive me for my inability to appreciate the path you've set them on and what you are doing in all our lives.

Forgiveness is a continual process, not a one-and-done act. I have to say it over and over. Asking and receiving forgiveness is one of the most healing and powerful acts of humanity.

Step 3: Gratitude, "Thank You"

Gratitude is something I struggle with. My mind is programmed to point out negative circumstances and emotions. One of my greatest gifts is being able to see what can be improved and helped to evolve, and it's also a source of frustration and judgment. I've been working on gratitude for many years in the form of gratitude journaling.

Saying "thank you" in the context of the Ho'oponopono prayer is one of the most impactful ways to grow in this area because you are practicing gratitude for something you are sorry for and need forgiveness. This very much ties into the praise prayer I discussed earlier. Here is how I might combine gratitude with praise:

- Thank you, Father, that love is more powerful than judgment. I praise you that I'm judgmental so I can feel what it's like and have empathy for others. Thank you that you do not judge us the same way humans judge each other.

- Thank you that pain moves us toward change and compassion. I praise you that we are able to feel pain and heal it by giving it to you. Thank you for sharing our pain and caring about us.

- Thank you for the feeling of jealousy so I can reflect on all that you have given me. Praise you for making me exactly the way I am and giving me all I need. Thank you for blessing them and helping me to share in their joy. Thank you for using their wealth for your purposes.

Step 4: Love, "I Love You"

The final step of "I love you" can be the first step and embedded into all the steps. You can say I love you to anything and everything—to yourself, your body, your soul, the air you breathe, the house that shelters you, the people and animals you love and those you hate, the systems that bind, and all your challenges, to name a few.

Love is the organizing force of the universe and is more powerful than we realize.[6] As spiritual entrepreneurs, our work is to grow love, so we send love in the practice of Ho'oponopono and in any other ways we can. We begin and end with love. The key is to keep saying it until you authentically feel love in your heart. Here is how I might end the prayers:

- Please send them love, Father. Fill them with love and fill me with your love so others may see you in me.

- Help me to love the education system despite the pain. Send compassion and love to everyone involved in the system. Help me to see that love somehow makes all the pain worth it in the end. Give me grace to bring love when I interact with this space.

- Help me to love those I'm envious of. Send them love right now and bless them, Father. Please fill their hearts with love so they have the courage to share your gifts. Fill me with love for all your children, including your enemies. Give me an opportunity to show them true love.

Typically, while saying Ho'oponopono, another topic arises to pray for, and I can continue this process for quite a long time. I find it is best to close by breathing in love and forgiveness for a few minutes and listening in silence.

---

[6] Quantum physics has several theories that support a force that interconnects us all. See Michael Talbot, *Beyond the Quantum* (Bantam, 1988) for more information (particularly chapter 3).

The Eight-Step Prayer

My husband, Scott, learned the eight-step prayer while in a hospital for two weeks after almost dying of pulmonary blood clots. The late Dr. Henry Wright developed this methodology to assist people in healing.[7] Dr. Wright guided chronically and terminally ill people through this prayer and many were healed. He felt such recoveries were *not* miracles, as the body would naturally heal itself if you corrected the environment fostering the disease. To this end, he reported success with people of all faiths and no particular faith.

After tens of thousands of case studies, Dr. Wright's data indicated a correlation between emotional states and disease in 85% of the cases. Certainly, there are a lot of factors that contribute to the condition of our health. Dr. Wright was especially interested in how emotional states affect the biochemistry of the body, which in turn fosters an environment conducive to the development of certain diseases. The eight-step prayer was his way of helping people out of the emotional states that lead to disease. Indeed, it is very hard for us to simply stop worrying or stop being bitter, angry, jealous, etc.

Scott and I use this prayer often in our relationship when we are fighting. It's the most powerful prayer we know for removing negative walls of emotion, which over time can be not only detrimental to our relationship but also to our health.

---

[7] Dr. Henry Wright, *A More Excellent Way* (Whitaker House, 2009).

Simply put, the eight-step prayer is comprised of the following components:

1. Recognize
2. Responsibility
3. Renounce
4. Repent
5. Reject
6. Resist
7. Restore
8. Rejoice

The eight-step prayer by Scott A. Smith

The following description of the prayer is based on my husband's own version of the eight-step prayer. I have edited it with his permission to align more closely with the concepts presented in this book.

There are no set words to the prayer. It is not a magical incantation. Instead, it is a tool for learning about yourself and a means to help grow. I have been amazed at how well the prayer works and at how different I feel after using the prayer. I have also been surprised at how stubborn I can be at harboring harmful feelings that are actually lies. I have gradually learned to feel the toxicity of certain mental states in my gut, in my heart, or coursing through my body. Recognizing that toxic feeling has become a clue that I need to clear a particular emotional state that is harming me.

The following description of each step is based upon my own experience. I blended the Ho'oponopono prayer and the praise prayer into these steps as they are powerful when used either separately or in combination.

Step One: Recognize

The first step is to recognize what we are doing that is not helpful. This can be as easy as admitting, "Father, I recognize I am angry." Or it can be as difficult as learning to recognize behaviors that may seem justified and have been normalized but are hurtful, harming both ourselves and those around us.

Thus, the first step of the eight-step prayer is to learn to recognize unhelpful behavior or thinking. We are prone to feeling that our perceptions are a true reflection of the way the world really is, when often they are not. Thus, we can end up feeling justified when we are engaged in harmful emotional states, in which case we continue blindly on, reinforcing our beliefs while harming ourselves and others.

It is astounding how differently we can perceive our world after praying. I once used the eight-step prayer when I was very overwhelmed. When I finished, I wondered if I'd forgotten all I needed to do, as I was no longer feeling overwhelmed. So, I carefully made a list, only to discover I had deceived myself into being overwhelmed. I had a full day ahead of me, but I could do everything I needed to.

As I mentioned above, I include Carothers's prayer of praise in step one, so the way to approach the first step is to say something like, "Father, I recognize that I am feeling ____. Praise you that I am feeling this way as I know you have a plan for this situation."

Here are a few of the many feelings you can put in the blank: angry, bitter, jealous, offended, outraged, afraid, depressed, defeated, self-pitying, lustful, greedy, incapable, despairing, paranoid, addicted, obsessed, hurt, unworthy, judgmental, and contemptuous.

Step Two: Responsibility

The second step is to take responsibility for what you are doing that is not helpful. If it is easy for us to feel that our feelings accurately reflect situations, it is even easier to feel that our responses are justified. We say, "Of course I am angry—I have been waiting in traffic for over an hour now!" or "Of course I am hurt—she had no right to say that!" It is very difficult to take responsibility for our feelings when we feel they are justified.[8]

The fact that we can learn to choose, even if it takes guidance and hard work, whether to move into this state or not is what makes humans unique. For me, being able to choose and take responsibility for our feelings, and how we react based on them, illustrates the true potential of our free will.

A way to approach the second step is to say something like, "I take responsibility for feeling offended. It's not something I can't help; it's something I'm responsible for."

Step Three: Renounce

The third step is to renounce that which you are doing as being unhelpful or unhealthy. You renounce the universal unhelpfulness or unhealthiness of the behavior or feeling. Essentially you are acknowledging that the feeling or the behavior is destructive to life itself. So, you can say something like, "I renounce contempt in my life and throughout the world. It is never helpful."

---

[8] Aaron Karim, "Anger and the Brain: What happens in your head when you get angry," *PsychCentral:* psychcentral.com (June 1, 2016).

Step Four: Repent

The fourth step is to repent or to commit to stop doing that which is unhelpful. In other words, if bitterness is destroying you, then repenting of bitterness is deciding to move away from bitterness for your own well-being. As I said above, I add the first two parts of the Ho'oponopono prayer here, too. Thus, you can say something like, "Father, I am sorry that I am bitter, please forgive me. I repent of feeling bitter. I no longer want to feel this way."

Step Five: Reject

The fifth step is to reject the spirit you allowed into your life. When we allow ourselves to become jealous, bitter, etc., we open our hearts to the dark forces within the spiritual world. In the fifth step you acknowledge the presence of the spirit you allowed into your life and you reject it. Thus, you can say something like, "Spirit of despair, I reject you in the name of God. I shall have nothing to do with you anymore, and you are no longer welcome in me."

If you are not comfortable in asking God or a higher power for help in this way, you can invoke your own will. As I have said, Dr. Wright found the process worked for people with many different spiritual beliefs.

Step Six: Resist

The sixth step is to pledge resistance when the feeling returns. This step recognizes that the process of growing stronger is an on-going process. Even after you learn to cast off the feeling of outrage, for example, it will return—only next time, it will give you a better excuse. Once you've learned to overcome feeling outraged when stuck in traffic, the next time someone intentionally cuts you off, you can practice another emotion instead, such as forgiveness, gratitude, or love. Thus, you can say something like, "Spirit of outrage, I shall resist you when you try to return, for as long as you return. There is no place for you in my heart anymore." Again, you can ask God for help with this.

Step Seven: Restore

The seventh step is to ask God to restore you to be as he intended you to be. In this seventh step, we use our free will to invite God into our hearts, and we give him permission to change us and restore us to the person he intended us to be. Note that this is an act of our free will, and that in doing so, we are choosing to align ourselves with the will of God. To do so, one can simply say, "God, I ask that you restore me to be the person you intended me to be."

Step Eight: Rejoice

The eighth step is to rejoice in your restoration. This step recognizes that you are living life exercising your free will and that in your journey you will make mistakes and go off target. When you do, you will hurt yourself and others, causing pain that can be a wake-up call. Your wake-up call can result in wisdom and lead to spiritual growth so that you have a greater measure of free will in the future. I add the last two steps of the Ho'oponopono prayer here. To rejoice, one simply says, "Father, I rejoice in your forgiveness! Thank you for your restoration. I love you very much."

Putting the eight-step prayer together

The eight-step prayer is quite long, but I find it a powerful structure that acts as a sort of mantra. Here is an example of all eight steps written out in one place:

1. **Recognize:** Father, I recognize that I am feeling judgmental. I praise you that I am feeling this way because it provides self-awareness and a chance to heal myself and that which I'm judging.

2. **Responsibility:** I take responsibility for feeling judgmental. It's my natural reaction, but I know judgment isn't true or helpful.

3. **Renounce:** I renounce judgement in my life and throughout the world. It is never my place to judge.

4. **Repent:** I am sorry that I am judgmental, please forgive me. I repent of feeling judgmental. I no longer want to feel this way.

5. **Reject:** Spirit of judgment, I reject you (you can add in the name of God/ Jesus). I shall have nothing to do with you anymore, and you are no longer welcome in my heart, mind, body or soul.

6. **Resist:** Spirit of judgment, I shall resist you when you try to return, for as long as you return. There is no place for you in my life anymore. I am replacing your judgmental influence with discernment and grace.

7. **Restore:** God, I ask that you restore me to be the person you intended me to be, my true self.

8. **Rejoice:** Father, I rejoice in your forgiveness. Thank you for your restoration. I love you very much.

Appendix III
Bibliography: Book and Article List

Aron, Elaine N. "The Highly Sensitive Person." https://hsperson.com/.

Academy of Ideas. "Søren Kierkegaard and the Value of Despair." October 19, 2020. https://academyofideas.com/2020/10/soren-kierkegaard-value-of-despair/.

Alfonso, Fernando. "$350 million for WeWork co-founder shows how broken and biased venture capital is." *National Public Radio*, August 26, 2022. https://www.npr.org/2022/08/26/1119415180/wework-flow-adam-neumann-vc-venture-capital-350-million-gender-bias-horowitz.

Ali, A.J. *L.O.V.E. Is the Answer.* https://trylovenow.com/.

Aron, Elaine N. *The Highly Sensitive Person.* Citadel Press, 1996.

Austin, Henry. "What are the 'twisties?' Simone Biles explains gymnastics struggle at Tokyo Olympics." *NBC News*, July 30, 2021. https://www.nbcnews.com/news/olympics/what-are-twisties-simone-biles-explains-gymnastics-struggle-tokyo-olympics-n1275460.

B Lab. "B Corporation: Welcome." B Corp. https://bcorporation.net/.

Baldwin, Christina and Ann Linnea. *The Circle Way: A Leader in Every Chair.* San Francisco: Berrett-Koehler Publishing, 2010. http://www.thecircleway.net/.

Bank of International Settlements. https://www.bis.org/.

Basics in Kabbalah and Chassidut: The Names of God – Havayah. Gal Einai: Revealing the Torah's Inner Dimension. https://www.inner.org/names/namhavay.htm.

BEMA Podcast. BEMA Discipleship. https://www.bemadiscipleship.com/.

Bertone, Holly J., CNHP, PMP and Crystal Hoshaw. "Which Type of Meditation Is Right for Me?" Updated November 5, 2021. *Healthline*. https://www.healthline.com/health/mental-health/types-of-meditation.

Boom, Corrie ten, Elizabeth Sherrill and John Sherrill. *The Hiding Place*. 35th ed. Grand Rapids: Chosen Books, 2006.

Brenna, Dan M.D. "What Are Mala Beads?" *WebMD*, October 23, 2021. https://www.webmd.com/balance/what-are-mala-beads.

Brower, Tracy. "Empathy Is the Most Important Leadership Skill According to Research." *Forbes*, September 19, 2021. https://www.forbes.com/sites/tracybrower/2021/09/19/empathy-is-the-most-important-leadership-skill-according-to-research/.

Brown, Brene. *Dare to Lead: Brave Work. Tough Conversations. Whole Hearts*. Vermilion: Random House, 2018

Brown, Brene. "Dare to Lead Hub." https://brenebrown.com/hubs/dare-to-lead/.

California Indian Education. "Crazy Horse/ Tashunca, Lakota." https://www.californiaindianeducation.org/famous_indian_chiefs/crazy_horse/.

Campbell, Joseph. *The Hero's Journey*. San Francisco: Harper & Row Publishers, 1990.

Carothers, Merlin. *Prison to Praise*. Escondido, CA: Merlin Carothers, 1970.

Carson, Rick. *Taming Your Gremlin*. Revised edition. New York: Quill, 2003.

Castrillon, Caroline. "5 Ways to Go from a Scarcity to Abundance Mindset."

Forbes, July 12, 2020. https://www.forbes.com/sites/carolinecastrillon/2020/07/12/5-ways-to-go-from-a-scarcity-to-abundance-mindset/.

Chetty, Raj, et.al. et.al., Opportunity Insights Team. "Social Capital and Economic Mobility." Non-technical Research Summary. *Opportunity Insights*, August, 2002. https://opportunityinsights.org/wp-content/uploads/2022/07/.

Co-Active Training Institute. "Leadership Training." *Co-Active Training*. https://coactive.com/training/leadership-training/.

Coelho, Paulo. *The Alchemist.* Later printing edition. Translated by Alan R. Clarke. San Francisco: HarperOne, 2005.

Coelho, Paulo. *The Pilgrimage.* Translated by Alan R. Clarke. San Francisco: HarperOne, 2008.

Covey, Steven. *The 7 Habits of Highly Effective People*. Miami: Mango Media, 2015.

De Saint-Exupery, Antoine. *The Little Prince*. Samaira Book Publishers, 2017.

"Developing Talent? You're probably Missing Vertical Development." Leading Effectively Article., *Center for Creative Leadership*. www.ccl.org/articles/.

Dusen, Wilson Van. *The Presence of Other Worlds: The Psychological/ Spiritual Findings of Emmanuel Swedenborg*. 2nd ed. West Chester: Chrysalis Books, 2004.

Eisenstein, Charles. "Volatility." *Charles Eisenstein* (blog), January 23, 2022. https://charleseisenstein.substack.com/p/volatility?s=r.

Fernando, Jason. "Return on Investment (ROI): How to Calculate It and What It Means." *Investopedia.* Updated on June 30, 2022. https://www.investopedia.com/terms/r/returnoninvestment.asp.

Fischer, James. *Navigating the Growth Curve.* Boulder: Growth Curve Press, 2006.

Ford-Grabowsky, Mary ed. *Sacred Voices: Essential Women's Wisdom through the Ages*. San Francisco: HarperOne, 2002.

Forhman, Rabbi David. "Yamim Noraim: Meaning & Significance." Aleph Beta Recording. Video. https://www.alephbeta.org/playlist/yamim-noraim-confusing-satan.

Frankl, Viktor. *Man's Search for Meaning*. Boston: Beacon Press, 2006.

Freeman, Tzvi. *The Book of Purpose: Meditation My Rebbe Taught Me*. Class One Press, 2010. Copyright and excerpt reprinted with permission of Chabad.org/7804.

Freeman, Tzvi. "What Is Tikkun Olam? What does Tikkun Olam mean, who came up with it, and how do I do it?" *Chabad*. June 15, 2017. https://www.chabad.org/library/article_cdo/aid/3700275/jewish/What-Is-Tikkun-Olam.htm.

Ganti, Akhilesh. "Angel Investor Definition and How It Works." *Investopedia*, March 22, 2022. https://www.investopedia.com/terms/a/angelinvestor.asp.

"GDP – Econlib." *Library of Economics and Liberty*. https://www.econlib.org/library/Topics/College/gdp.html.

Gerson, Michael. "Opinion: Trump should fill Christians with rage. How come he doesn't." *The Washington Post*, September 01, 2022. https://www.washingtonpost.com/opinions/2022/09/01/michael-gerson-evangelical-christian-maga-democracy/.

Giannobile, Monica. "What is a Teal Organization?" *Workology*, February 17, 2022. https://workology.com/what-is-a-teal-organization/.

Gleeson, Susan M.D. *We Are Already Whole: A Book of Reflections and Invitations*. Independently Published, 2021.

Glick, Rabbi Yoel. *Living the Life of Jewish Meditation: A Comprehensive Guide to Practice and Experience*. 1st edition. Woodstock: Jewish Lights, 2014.

Glick, Rabbi Yoel. "Shavuot: Touching the Infinite and Eternal." Medium, June

03, 2022. https://medium.com/daat-elyon/touching-the-infinite-and-eternal.

Global Impact Investing Network. "What You Need to Know About Impact Investing." https://thegiin.org/impact-investing/need-to-know/.

Gruman, Galen. "Minority tech startups in the US have seen almost no progress in VC funding." *ComputerWorld*. October 07, 2020. https://www.computerworld.com/article/3584734/minority-tech-startups-in-the-us-have-seen-almost-no-progress-in-vc-funding.html.

Hamstra, Rachel. "The Trouble with Belly Breathing." *Rachel Hamstra, GCFP Blog*, December 08, 2017. https://www.rachelhamstra.com/blog/2017/12/6/the-trouble-with-belly-breathing.

Hartman, Robert S. *Freedom to Live: The Robert Hartman Story*. Edited by Arthur R. Ellis. 2nd edition. Wipf and Stock, 2013.

Hathaway, Ian. "What Startup Accelerators Really Do." *Harvard Business Review*, March 01, 2016. https://hbr.org/2016/03/what-startup-accelerators-really-do.

Hayes, Adam. "Hockey Stick Chart." *Investopedia*, updated October 23, 2021. https://www.investopedia.com/terms/h/hockey-stick-chart.asp.

Henley, Dede. "Research Says Vertical Development Can Make You a Better Leader." *Forbes*. January 31, 2020. https://www.forbes.com/sites/.

Henriques, Marth. "Can the legacy of trauma be passed down the generations?" *BBC*, March 26, 2019. https://www.bbc.com/future/article/20190326-what-is-epigenetics.

Hodges, Cassie Ann. "US Venture Capital Investment Surpasses $130 Billion in 2019 for Second Consecutive Year." National Ventura Capital Association, January 14, 2022. https://nvca.org/pressreleases/us-venture-capital-investment-surpasses-130-billion-in-2019-for-second-consecutive-year/.

Homer. *Iliad*. London: New York: Dent; Dutton, 1955.

Indigo Education Company. https://www.indigoeducationcompany.com/.

"Integral Theory." Wikipedia. Last modified September 17, 2022.
https://en.wikipedia.org/wiki/Integral_theory_(Ken_Wilber).

Iqbal, Mansoor. "Fortnite Usage and Revenue Statistics (2022)." *Business of Apps*, updated September 06, 2022.
https://www.businessofapps.com/data/fortnite-statistics/.

Jeanne Guyon, Jeanne. *Experiencing the Depths of Jesus Christ*. Beaumont, TX: The Seedsowers, 1975.

Keating, Thomas Keating. *The Mystery of Christ: The Liturgy as Spiritual Experience*. Continuum: 1994.

Keller, Hellen. *My Religion*. New York: Swedenborg Foundation, 1974.

Kimsey-House, Karen and Henry Kimsey-House. *Co-Active Leadership: Five Ways to Lead*. Oakland: Berrett-Koehler Publishers, Inc., 2015.

Klein, Josh. *You Are the Product*. St. Martin's Griffin, 2015.

Koch, Richard Koch. *The 80/20 Principle*. New York: Doubleday, 2008.

Kotashev, Kyril. "Startup Failure Rate: How Many Startups Fail and Why?" *Failory's Blog,* updated January 09, 2022.
https://www.failory.com/blog/startup-failure-rate.

Laloux, Frederic. "The Future of Management is Teal." *Strategy+Business*. July 06, 2015. https://www.strategy-business.com/article/00344.

Laloux, Frederic. *Reinventing Organizations: A Guide to Creating Organizations Inspired by the Next Stage in Human Consciousness*. Foreword by Ken Wilber. Nelson Parker, 2014.

Lee, Jenna. "What is a cap table?" *The Carta Blog*, October 08, 2019.
https://carta.com/blog/what-is-a-cap-table/.

Leibert, Elizabeth. *The Way of Discernment*. Westminster John Knox Press, 2008.

Levy, Paul. *Wetiko: Healing the Mind-Virus That Plagues Our World*. Forward by Larry Dossey, M.D. Inner Traditions, 2021.

Lewis, Clive Staples. *The Screwtape Letters*. Reprint edition. HarperOne, 2015.

Liminal Space. "What is a Liminal Space." In A Liminal Space. https://www.inaliminalspace.org/about-us/what-is-a-liminal-space.

MacMahon, Brian. "The Kidnapping of the American Dream." July 19, 2016. University of California Irvine. TEDx Talks. Video. https://www.youtube.com/watch?v=Y6f7lFy0oW0.

Maldonado, Camilo. "Price of College Increasing Almost 8 Times Faster Than Wages." *Forbes*, July 24, 2018. https://www.forbes.com/sites/camilomaldonado/2018/07/24/price-of-college-increasing-almost-8-times-faster-than-wages/.

Malik, Daniyal. "How Big Tech Companies Are Earning Billions To Beat The Economy of Whole Countries." *Digital Information World*, August 25, 2020. https://www.digitalinformationworld.com/2020/08/how-big-tech-companies-are-earning-billions-to-beat-the-economy-of-big-countries.html.

Mathur, Priyamvada. "Six charts that show 2021's record year for US venture capital." *Pitchbook*, January 19, 2022. https://pitchbook.com/news/articles/2021-record-year-us-venture-capital-six-charts#.

McLaren, Karla. *The Language of Emotions*. Boulder: Sounds True, 2010.

Milton Hershey School. "About   Explore MHS History." Milton Hershey School. https://www.mhskids.org/about.

Mitchell, Sherri. *Sacred Instructions: Indigenous Wisdom for Living Spirit-Based Change*. North Atlantic Books, 2018.

Muller, Wayne. *Sabbath: Finding Rest, Renewal, and Delight In Our Busy Lives*. Bantam Books, 1999.

Myrick, Christin. *Your Fearless Soul*. Birdhouse Publishing LLC, 2015.

http://yourfearlesssoul.com/.

Nadworny, Elissa. "Does It Matter Where You Go To College? Some Context for the Admissions Scandal." *National Public Radio*, March 13, 2019. https://www.npr.org/2019/03/13/702973336/does-it-matter-where-you-go-to-college-some-context-for-the-admissions-scandal.

Nakao, Roshi Egyoku. "The Three Tenets." *Zen Peacemakers International*. https://zenpeacemakers.org/the-three-tenets/.

Newell, J Philip. *The Book of Creation: An Introduction to Celtic Spirituality* Novalis, 1999.

Orloff, Judith. *The Empath's Survival Guide*. Sounds True, 2017.

PBS. "Seven Generations – the Role of Chief." https://www.pbs.org/warrior/content/timeline/opendoor/roleOfChief.html.

Pico della Mirandola, Giovanni. *Oration on the Dignity of Man*. Gateway Editions, 1996.

Plotkin, Bill. *Nature and the Human Soul: Cultivating Wholeness and Community in a Fragmented World.* Novato: New World Library, 2008.

Plotkin, Bill. *Soulcraft Crossing into the Mysteries of Nature and Psyche.* New World Library, 2003.

Pressfield, Steven. *The War of Art: Break Through the Blocks and Win Your Inner Creative Battles.* New York: Black Irish Entertainment, 2012.

Rohr, Richard. "Fully Human." Center for Action and Contemplation. May 16, 2016. https://cac.org/fully-human-2016-05-16/.

Rohr, Richard. "The Zealots and the Pharisees." Center for Action and Contemplation, July 12, 2022. https://cac.org/daily-meditations/the-zealots-and-the-pharisees-2022-07-12/ .

Rohr, Richard. *Immortal Diamond: The Search for Our True Self.* San Francisco: Jossey-Bass, 2013.

Rose, Todd. "The Myth of Average." Filmed June 20, 2013. Sonoma County, CA. TEDx Talks video. https://www.youtube.com/watch?v=4eBmyttcfU4.

Roth, Gabrielle. "5Rhythms." 5Rhythms. https://www.5rhythms.com/.

Ruiz, Don Miguel. *The Four Agreements: A Practical Guide to Personal Freedom*. Amber-Allen Publishing, Incorporated, 1997.

Schulweis, Harold. "Echad Rosha Hashana, 1997." Valley Beth Shalom. https://www.vbs.org/worship/meet-our-clergy/rabbi-harold-schulweis/sermons/echad.

Schwartz, Stephen. *Wicked: a New Musical: Original Broadway Cast Recording*. New York, NY: Decca Broadway, 2003.

Scott, MacKenzie. "Seeding by Ceding." *Medium*, June 15, 2021. https://mackenzie-scott.medium.com/seeding-by-ceding-ea6de642bf.

Smith, Scott A. *The Emerging Kingdom: An Economic Guidebook to Building a Nation that is a Better Place to Live*. Independently published, 2021.

Smith, Scott Andrew. *A Tale of Two Economies: A New Financial Operating System for the American Economy* (Independently published, 2022).

Smith, Summer. *The Blue Journal*. Scotts Valley: CreateSpace, 2015.

SOCAP Global. "About Us - SOCAP Global." *SOCAP Global*: https://socapglobal.com/about-us/.

Solomon, Marty and Brent Billings. "Galatians – Two Women, Two Covenants." *BEMA Discipleship Podcast Episode 147*, December 12, 2019. Podcast. MP3 Audio. https://www.bemadiscipleship.com/147.

Solomon, Marty and Brent Billings. "Jewish Hermeneutics." March 28, 2019, in *BEMA Discipleship Podcast Episode 110*. Podcast. MP3 Audio. https://www.bemadiscipleship.com/110.

Spiral Dynamics Integral. "Integral Theory." Spiral Dynamics Integral Nederland. https://spiraldynamicsintegral.nl/en/about-sdi/integral-theory/.

St. George Donna, and Valerie Strauss. "The crisis of student mental health is much vaster than we realize." *Washington Post*. December 5, 2022. https://www.washingtonpost.com/education/

Swedenborg Center. "Church of the Holy City: Spiritual Growth, Dialogue and Community." Church of the Holy City. https://holycitydc.org/.

Swedenborg, Emmanuel. *Heaven and Hell*. Translated by John C. Ager. Start Publishing: 2012. Scribd.

Swedenborg, Emmanuel. *Heaven and its Wonder and Hell*. Translated by George F. Dole. West Chester: Swedenborg Foundation, 2000.

Tabachnick, Cara. "Here's what you should know before attending a whirling dervish ceremony in Turkey." *The Washington Post*. April 12, 2019. https://www.washingtonpost.com/lifestyle/travel/heres-what-you-should-know-before-attending-a-whirling-dervish-ceremony-in-turkey/.

Talbot, Michael. *Beyond the Quantum*. Bantam, 1988

Talent Recap. "Voices of The City "Homeless" Choir Get Terry Crews GOLDEN BUZZER!" May 27, 2020. Video, 4:57 min. https://www.youtube.com/watch?v=-tAyPwL-JCI.

Tardi, Carla. "The 80-20 Rule (aka Pareto Principle): What It Is, How It Works." *Investopedia*, updated July 07, 2022. https://www.investopedia.com/terms/1/80-20-rule.asp.

Target Training International, Ltd. "Research-Baked Assessments." TTI Success Insights. https://www.ttisi.com/.

TED Foundation. "TEDx Talks | Watch | TED." TED. https://www.ted.com/watch/tedx-talks.

The Foundation for a Better Economy. "The Emerging Kingdom – Financial Freedom Act." https://www.thefoundationforabettereconomy.org/.

Tolle, Eckhart. *The Power of Now*. London, England: Hodder Paperback, 2001.

Tontonoz, Matthew. "What Is Epigenetics, and Why Is Everyone Talking about It?" *Memorial Sloan Kettering Cancer Center*, June 19, 2018. https://www.mskcc.org/news/what-epigenetics-and-why-everyone-talking-about-it.

Toshalis, Eric, and Virgel Hammonds. "Let's Face It: Tracking Is Intentional Systemic Inequity." *KnowledgeWorks*, November 02, 2021. https://knowledgeworks.org/resources/tracking-is-intentional-systemic-inequity/.

Tuchman, Lauren. "The Shekhinah or the Divine Presence or Divine Feminine in Judaism." *State of Formation*, January 18, 2012. https://stateofformation.org/2012/01/the-shekhinah-or-the-divine-presence-or-divine-feminine-in-judaism/.

Tuovila, Alicia. "Pro Forma: What It Means and How to Create Pro Forma Financial Statements." *Investopedia*, August 20, 2022. https://www.investopedia.com/terms/p/proforma.asp.

Twist, Lynn. *The Soul of Money: Reclaiming the Wealth of Our Inner Resources.* W.W. Norton & Company, 2006.

United States Holocaust Memorial Museum. Holocaust Encyclopedia. https://encyclopedia.ushmm.org/en.

Van der Kolk, Bessel A. *The Body Keeps the Score: Brain, Mind, and Body in the Healing of Trauma.* Penguin, 2015.

Vitale, Joe, and Ihaleakala Hew Len. *Zero Limits: The Secret Hawaiian System for Wealth, Health, Peace, and More.* 1st ed. Wiley, 2009.

Voice of Our City Organization. "San Diego Homeless Choir - Choir for Homeless." https://www.voicesofourcity.org/.

Wachowski, Lana, and Lilly Wachowski dir. *The Matrix*. United States: Warner Bros, 1999.

WebMD Editorial Contributors. "What Is Scarcity Mentality?" Reviewed by Dan Brennan, MD. *WebMD*, updated October 25, 2021. https://www.webmd.com/mental-health/what-is-scarcity-mentality.

Wentworth, Brenda LCSW. "Home." Counseling and Therapy in Boulder County, Longmont, CO. https://www.brendawentworth.com/.

"What is co-creation?" *Fronteer*. https://fronteer.com/what-is-co-creation/.

Wiley, Eleanor and Maggie Oman. *A String and a Prayer: How to make and use prayer beads.* Boston, MA: Red Wheel/Weiser, 2002.

Wright, Henry W. *A More Excellent Way: Be in Health.* New Kensington: Whitaker House, 2009.

Yale, Aly J. "What to know about the scarcity mindset and how it affects women and their finances — and 6 ways to avoid it." *Business Insider*, May 07, 2022. https://www.businessinsider.com/personal-finance/scarcity-mindset.

ABOUT THE AUTHOR

Sheri Smith is the founder and CEO of Indigo, an organization that envisions people-centered systems that cultivate self-awareness, empathy, and freedom. With over two decades of experience in developing assessment technology for businesses as well as for secondary and post-secondary education environments, Sheri is passionate about helping people find their voice.

During her college years, Sheri interned for Vital Voices, a global women's rights initiative, where she discovered her passion for empowering people. She shifted her career focus to consulting and saw the benefits of clients' work aligning with their true selves.

Sheri founded Indigo with a vision to create a lifelong education system that empowers individuals to live their purpose, shifting away from standardization. Indigo includes three entities: 1) an education technology company, 2) a non-profit arm focused on economic development, and 3) a free job-seeker web application, IndigoPathway.com.

Sheri received her B.A. in International Studies from American University and her M.A. in Communication, Culture and Technology (CCT) from Georgetown University.

www.ingramcontent.com/pod-product-compliance
Lightning Source LLC
Chambersburg PA
CBHW031614210526
45464CB00004B/1575